# Women in Christ

*From the Fire to the Table!*

Compiled by Traci Vanderbush

Contributors: Amber Twigg, Becky Bird, Bethany Martin, Bettina Grzeskowiak, Bonnie Goolsby, Brit Eaton, Britany Bloom, Carrie Cole, Celeste Keplin-Weeks, Cheryl Ricker, Christine Zucker, Danielle Babin, Eve Passmore, Hannah Wakeman, Jeanne Kaufman, Jennifer Hart Shaw, Katie Thorpe, Kayla Carrier Santos, Kayla Roberts, Kerry Walker, Kristin Tucker, Libby Higgins, Michelle Carrier, Regis Blalock, Robin Hertz Hempel, Ronda Olson, Ronda Vanderbush, Sally Hanan, Sarah Morales, Shana Orser, Shirley Peschell, Stefanie Monk, Stephanie Tate, Tiffany Matthews, Traci Vanderbush.

Copyright © 2024 by Traci Vanderbush. All rights to the individual stories are held by their respective authors.

Title: Women in Christ: From the Fire to the Table! / Compiled by Traci A. Vanderbush

Printed in the United States of America.

All rights reserved. No part of this publication may be reproduced, distributed, or transmitted in any form or by any means, including photocopying, recording, or other electronic or mechanical methods, without the prior written permission of from the copyright holders, except in the case of brief quotations embodied in critical reviews and certain other noncommercial uses permitted by copyright law. For permission requests, write to tracivanderbush@gmail.com.

Publisher's Note: The stories contained in this compilation are personal narratives reflecting the lived experiences of women who have faced significant challenges and hardships. The authors have shared their truths with the intention of giving encouragement and hope. While the narratives may evoke strong emotions and touch upon sensitive topics, including trauma, loss, and resilience, they are not intended to serve as universal representations of all women's experiences.

Ordering Information: Special discounts are available on quantity purchases by corporations, associations, and others. For details, contact the publisher at the email address above.

Scripture quotations (unless otherwise noted) taken from the New American Standard Bible® (NASB), Copyright © 1960, 1962, 1963, 1968, 1971, 1972, 1973, 1975, 1977, 1995 by The Lockman Foundation. Used by permission. www.Lockman.org.

Scripture quotations marked (AMP) are taken from *The Amplified ® Bible*, Copyright © 1954, 1958, 1962, 1964, 1965, 1987, by the Lockman Foundation. Used by permission. (www.Lockman.org.) All rights reserved.

Scripture quotations marked (ESV) are from The Holy Bible, English Standard Version ® (ESV ®), copyright © 2001 by Crossway, a publishing ministry of Good News Publishers. Used by permission. All rights reserved.

Scripture quotations marked (KJV) are from the Authorized (King James) Version. Rights in the Authorized Version in the United Kingdom are vested in the Crown. Reproduced by permission of the Crown's patentee, Cambridge University Press.

Scripture quotations marked (MSG) are from *The Message*. Copyright © by Eugene H. Peterson 1993, 1994, 1995, 1996, 2000, 2001, 2002. Used by permission of Tyndale House Publishers, Inc.

Scripture quotations marked (NIV) are taken from the Holy Bible, New International Version®, NIV®. Copyright © 1973, 1978, 1984, 2011 by Biblica, Inc.™ Used by permission of Zondervan. All rights reserved worldwide. www.zondervan.com. The "NIV" and "New International Version" are trademarks registered in the United States Patent and Trademark Office by Biblica, Inc.™

Scripture marked (NKJV) are taken from the New King James Version ®. Copyright © 1982 by Thomas Nelson. Used by permission. All rights reserved.

Scripture quotations marked (NLT) are taken from the *Holy Bible, New Living Translation*, copyright © 1996, 2004, 2007, 2013 by Tyndale House Foundation. Used by permission of Tyndale House Publishers, Inc., Carol Stream, Illinois 60188. All rights reserved.

Scripture quotations marked (TPT) are from The Passion Translation®. Copyright © 2017, 2018 by Passion & Fire Ministries, Inc. Used by permission. All rights reserved. ThePassionTranslation.com.

Typesetting: Inksnatcher.com
Cover design: Lesia T.

Print ISBN: 9798343234985

Profits from this project will go to support various nonprofit organizations that empower women in Christ.

*To all the women who are ready
to let their voices be heard.*

# Contents

Women at the Roundtable ................................................. i
And So We Began. .......................................................... iii
The Woman's Perfect Diet, Our Daily Bread ................... 1
A Testimony... or a Test of Money ................................... 5
Fight the Good Fight of Faith ......................................... 10
From Death to Life (and Back Again) ............................ 16
In the Lights of New York City ...................................... 21
But I'm Right! ................................................................. 26
Sitting in Sadness ............................................................ 31
Freedom from Panic Attacks .......................................... 35
God Sent a Bus! .............................................................. 40
I Choose Him .................................................................. 44
The Unbeatable Power ................................................... 47
The Redemptive Work in the Midst of Trauma ............. 51
God's Plan A ................................................................... 54
Out in the Waters ............................................................ 59
A Supernatural Experience ............................................. 62
My Peach Story ............................................................... 65
Being Present in His Presence ........................................ 68
Do It for Me .................................................................... 74
Snakes in the Fire ............................................................ 77
The Power of a Story ...................................................... 81
Healed and Delivered ..................................................... 86
Spiritual Grit ................................................................... 92

| | |
|---|---|
| Carrying Promise | 96 |
| It's Never Too Late! | 100 |
| Embrace the Journey | 104 |
| Mailbox Massacre | 108 |
| The Eye of the Beholder | 112 |
| Cotton Panties | 116 |
| The Knowing | 124 |
| From Addiction to Freedom | 129 |
| Dismantling Panic | 136 |
| Who Am I? | 139 |
| Hot Mess to Destiny | 143 |
| Happiness Indeed | 146 |
| Windows, Doors, and Jail Cells | 150 |
| Walk On | 155 |
| A Pause | 157 |
| About the Author | 161 |
| Contributors | 162 |
| Acknowledgments | 164 |

# Women at the Roundtable

Dear Women,

I have had an ache in my heart for many years. It is hard to explain the little twinge deep inside that stirs up my dreamy notions of building a long wooden table that stretches across a vast field of green—a place where I invite you to come and sit, to be served all the tasty delicacies of life, while pampering you with gifts to soothe and refresh. I imagine towering trees on either side of the table framing a sunset in the distance. I hear the sounds of healing music being played over you, the kind that comforted King Saul when David played his harp. On the table are baskets of fruit and the richest fat-burning chocolates (I believe there is such a thing in the kingdom), where the most amazing mocktails and teas are highlighted by the golden hour. And, of course, wines for my wine connoisseurs.

One by one, each of you stands up to speak, to let your voice be heard, speaking of the glories and goodness found in the moment, having gone from the fire to the table, risen from the ash heap and now seated with princes (Psalm 113:7–8).

We bask in the light of deliverance and stories of being carried through circumstances that sought to devastate us. We would tell each other, "You've got this because God's got this. Christ is in you. The hope of glory lives inside you. I see you. I see your pain. I hear you. You are not alone. God's love never fails. We are together in this. We've got your back. It's okay to cry for a while. Joy comes in the morning. There's a promise on the horizon and it's greater than we can imagine."

We turn to look at the setting sun as the crushing weight of trials and challenges melts away in the orange, gold, pink, and purple hues of God's creative hand. Where grace is inhaled and gratitude is released in the atmosphere. Where we count one another to be a hero on some level. We are overcomers, more than conquerors through Christ.

*Women in Christ*

But since I don't yet have a field and I don't yet have that long, amazing table, I have invited a few women in my life to let their voices be heard in the pages of this book. Just for you! This is my way of creating the moment I have envisioned for many years, yet there are millions more who should be sitting at the table. I am not here to try to write a bestseller or professional book. If I was, it would take much longer to get this work perfected and published. I am here, just like you, in the midst of a busy life, to create a space where we can gather. Until we get to meet in person, this book will be a companion to you where you will find hope, encouragement, and life-giving words that let you know you are not alone.

So here, instead of at a long table, envision a women's roundtable where you can lean into the conversation. From the magnificent setting of creation to the interior of a room for intimate conversation, imagine all the goodness of God enveloping you as we gather next to a fire. Warm and inviting. This "table" will remain on these pages, ready for you to pick up any day or any time when you need encouragement. The topics vary from testimonies to life lessons to tragedies lived through, so you will find words of hope and life on any page.

Welcome to the table.

With all my heart,

*Traci Vanderbush*

# And So We Began…

In the hidden place, the silent, secret darkness. In a seeming void, life appeared; a cell infused with life, meeting with other cells; creating, moving, pulsing, working together. Carried. Held. And then…

Thrust into the light, the brightness, chaos, and sound. Where air meets skin, where breath is breathed for the first time. Once enveloped in warmth, now showing face to a world in which we vulnerably dwell. Defenseless and tiny, dependent upon the embrace of someone to clothe and feed us, and hopefully love us into the fullness of a destiny yet to be seen.

If you are reading these words, you have been born into this world. A woman, a mighty seed, making her mark on history. Whether big or small, seen or unseen, you are truly known and never alone. If you have been around this planet for a few decades, you have become familiar with pain, grief, highs and lows, valleys and mountains—which all come together to form who you are today. Perhaps you love who you have become. Perhaps you despise the woman you see in the mirror. If the latter, I pray you will feel differently as you read this book. In it you will hear many voices much like yours. There's power in women talking, and there's power in listening. So we come from the fire to the table.

But who are we?

For you have died, and your life is hidden with Christ in God (Colossians 3:3; Romans 6:8). You were made in the secret place (Psalm 139:15) to dwell in the shadow of your Maker (Psalm 91:1). In other words, your life began with the intimate weaving of the Creator's hands, face-to-face, together, hidden in beauty, filled with breath, to live and move and have your being, to lodge with the Divine. Christ took us with Him in His death and raised us up with Him in resurrection. How magnificent!

So as one—creating, moving, pulsing, and working in God's rest; where air meets skin and sacred, heavenly transfusion takes place—*we are the home of God*. It is clear: "Do you not know that your body is a temple of the Holy Spirit within you, whom you have from God, and that you are not your own?" (1 Corinthians 6:19). When women (temples of the Holy Spirit) come together to raise each other up, we are like the richest of mansions, filled with wisdom, power, and glory. What a perfect picture of the heart of the Father.

> In that union, He speaks to us and those in our presence as "My Beloved."

So, beloved, we are gathered here to encourage one another through this life we have been given. I invite you into this book where women's hearts unite in sharing their experiences, thoughts, and revelations to empower you. Come and feast on the richness of this sisterhood in Christ.

# The Table

Isn't it interesting that Jesus, God in the flesh, chose the profession of carpentry? He could have chosen a different family to be born into. Being God, He could have chosen any occupation and excelled in that role, yet God went low. Implanting Himself in the womb of a teenager who was not yet married, He began His walk as a man in the most scandalous way. In God's brilliance and perfection, He chose a way that seemed ignorant and imperfect to humanity. All of this to say, instead of choosing a powerful, professional, or highly regarded clerical position that would gain Him accolades, He followed in Joseph's footsteps and acquired the skills of a carpenter. Lowly birth, lowly worker, lowly death. Yet supremely the All-Sufficient One.

# And So We Began ...

I like to imagine that He made many tables in His carpentry days. The very One who was there before the foundation of the world, the Maker of trees, crafting, sanding, and feeling the wood with fingers of flesh. Did He smile as He created a place for humans to sit, to dine, and to commune with one another? Did His heart feel warm at the thought? "I go to prepare a place for you," He said to His disciples. But before He did that, He prepared places for people to come together and talk.

I wonder if He carved His name into one of His table creations. "Behold, I have inscribed you on the palms of My hands," God said (Isaiah 49:16). It is an incredible love that compels one to "tattoo" or engrave a name into their palm. I can only imagine that as Jesus carefully fashioned once-living trees into pedestals for mankind, He was engraving us into His own heart. And there He invited us to come to the table before we were ever born.

# The Woman's Perfect Diet

## Our Daily Bread

### Traci Vanderbush

Women are consumed with diet. We are inundated with ads and commercials that wash through our psyche, pressing our attention toward our weight and imperfections. As a woman who's in a post-menopausal phase, I've felt like a pinball in a machine, bouncing back and forth between pings of "Do this," "Don't do that," "Eat this," "Never eat that," and "You need this." It is frustrating beyond belief. If someone viewed my YouTube searches for exercise, they'd see the struggle: "Hey, Siri, find exercises to help with menopause." Exercise to burn fat, exercise to help hurting joints, exercise to help with urinary tract infections, stretches to release stress, breathing methods for calming … on and on it goes.

The worst part is that food seems to have become our enemy. Instead of feeling childlike joy over the excitement of eating, we often approach meals cautiously, as if they could be rattlesnakes waiting to bite. I recently realized that I'd lost joy and gratitude for the food set before me. I regarded it as a potential enemy. Though I chose healthy options, there was an element of shame and doubt that clouded my ability to consume provision with joy. I began to recall the happy feelings I had as a child when it was mealtime. Where had the delight gone? I decided to ask God to speak to me regarding food, and my perspective began to shift. He drew me back to a prayer I'd learned as a child. Here is what I learned.

# The Lord's Prayer

Have the words in what you call the Lord's Prayer become like a mantra to you? What I am talking about is how we tend to allow things to become mere phrases or repeated methods of tradition that eventually lose meaning to us. We may say the words, but the heart and mind have disconnected from the power in and behind the words.

As a little child, I learned to recite the Lord's Prayer, Psalm 23, John 3:16, and all the basics. It has taken over four decades for the meaning and power of the words to unfold and reveal themselves to me (thank you, Holy Spirit). As the child of a very young couple who struggled to make ends meet, when I prayed "Give us this day our daily bread," I felt like a beggar who was learning to trust in God's provision so we wouldn't go hungry. What a limited perspective that was! My parent's faith in God allowed me to see that He works miracles. Groceries were always there! Thankfully, throughout the years, I learned the deeper meaning of the prayer.

The most recent revelation of this prayer came to me through a dear and very intelligent friend of mine, Kayla Roberts. Her first language is Greek, so she reads the New Testament in Greek. She explained to me that the English language lacks much in regard to understanding the Scriptures. One of those areas that seems to be lacking in our English Bible translations is in the very verse we read as "Give us this day our daily bread." The original translation, as it was written so long ago is, "Give us this day the great I AM bread." Wow! The I

# The Woman's Perfect Diet, Our Daily Bread

AM, the Bread of Life Himself, the light of the world, the fullness, our source, the master Creator, the giver of breath!

Remember the story of Christ's temptation? When the devil tried to tempt Jesus in the wilderness, "[Jesus] answered, 'It is written, "Man shall not live by bread alone, but by every word that comes from the mouth of God"'" (Matthew 4:4 ESV). This is a message to us. We try to live by so many things, whether food, money, career, insurance, or strategies, but the truth is that it is all nothing if we are not consuming the very words of God. The very breath that was breathed into humanity is the breath of the great I AM. Without that infusion, we die. What God exhales never dies but grows, expands, and awakens eternally. When God said, "Let there be," I am convinced that creation never stopped. Even scientists know the universe is expanding.

I recently watched a film called *Deep Sky*, in which NASA scientists were interviewed about what they are seeing with today's technology. Tears filled my eyes as I watched two of the scientists fight back tears while describing what is far, far beyond what we ever knew to be. One said, "It's like seeing where we came from." Another, with wet eyes of wonder, said, "Eventually we will get to see the beginning of light." That Light spoke and life emerged, transformed, and continues to move. Imagine the endless power of words breathed by God. In those words are life and sustenance for our bodies, souls, and minds.

So now when I pray "Give us this day our daily bread," I know it is not an act of begging for mere human sustenance. It is the opening myself up to receive the breath and words that God has for me that day. Being Spirit led is the daily act of consuming the great I AM bread. In a world that is stopped up, junked up, and backed up by human opinions, accusations, and judgments, we can choose to lift our gaze, open our lungs, and breathe in deep the very words of God.

As you wake up each day, knowing His mercies are new every morning, shut out the noise, stretch out your arms, and ask to hear what God has to say. "Give us this day the great I AM bread." No longer a mantra. No longer cliché. It is life.

My journey into that prayer has restored to me the joy and gratitude of eating! As women, we must live according to God's voice day by day. Our lives depend on it. Instead of beating ourselves up over decision-making and feeling the weight of life choices, there is delight in sitting at His feet and letting the Spirit lead. Some days He may say, "Have that ice cream" and sometimes it might be, "Eat the blueberries instead."

There's a freedom that comes in being able to push aside the noise of thousands of articles and videos that try to tell you what is right for you. Leaning into childlike delight in being with God and following His lead is so much better! Each day becomes an adventure instead of a monotonous schedule to be followed. In Him is the woman's perfect diet.

Traci Vanderbush

# A Testimony ... or a Test of Money

### Becky Bird

One of the greatest challenges we face in life is money issues. Whether it is the love of money or lack of money, we have to decide to master it and not let it master us. I was born to a sixteen-year-old girl. My mom and dad worked hard to provide, but we knew financial lack at times, so I was used to doing without the name-brand items my classmates donned. They made fun of me when I attempted to make my clothes look like theirs.

I was familiar with phrases like "We could never afford that." "We cannot have that." "We cannot do that." It wasn't until later in adulthood that God began peeling away the poverty mindset I had developed—little by little, layer by layer—until I could finally live believing for the impossible despite what my bank account said. It has been a wild, wild adventure ever since. Not always easy but stunning.

My father-in-law, who once knew great poverty, used to remind us of the scripture that says we have never seen the righteous forsaken. "I have been young and now I am old, yet I have not seen the righteous forsaken or his descendants begging for bread" (Psalm 37:25). Those are encouraging words! On the flip side, "'what does it benefit a person to gain the whole world, and forfeit his soul?'" (Mark 8:36). It is clear we can go wrong and become unfruitful if we allow our trust and hope to be in money. I love the story that my wonderful friend Becky Bird shares about her experience with money. She is a successful businesswoman and former teacher who carries an energy and optimism I desire to harness. She brilliantly titled her story "A Testimony … or a Test of Money." I believe any of us can identify with her.

---∞---

Many years ago, I served as coordinator of children's ministry in a Pennsylvania Presbyterian church. It was the church where I was baptized, Joe and I were married, and our children were baptized and raised in a Christian upbringing.

When I began in the ministry, our church had an older congregation with few young families. As a staff, we prayed fervently for younger couples to accept Christ into their lives and to come into our church family. Within six months, we went from having twenty-plus children in the children's ministry program to over 120 children. That presented both new challenges and opportunities for God to change my life in particular.

The church had a large basement that was being leased to Head Start. They permanently rented one half of the space for their classrooms. The other half with the fellowship hall was used only for their activity space as this was also used by the church. Every Friday evening, I set up the fellowship hall with furniture, portable dividers, and teaching supplies to create classroom space. Then every Sunday afternoon, this all needed to be dismantled. As a church, we soon realized that we needed to reclaim the rented Head Start area for the growing children's ministry.

During the process of the church growth, I oversaw plans for creating permanent classrooms in the basement. I met with contractors, priced building materials, and sought

# A Testimony ... or a Test of Money

commitments from skilled men within the congregation to offset some of the contract labor cost. With the information compiled, I had a cost projection for the project. I began praying daily that the money needed for the project would be donated.

During that month, our house was burglarized. All of my jewelry was stolen. My biggest personal weakness was fine jewelry. Since childhood, my parents had marked every special occasion—birthday, Christmas, and vacation—with a gift of jewelry. When Joe and I married, he continued that tradition. I was heartbroken and angry with God that my jewelry was stolen. I cried out to Him, pleading, "Why my jewelry?" Joe and I were faithful tithers. In addition, I also donated all my church salary and then some back into the church. But God knew my heart. He told me I had held onto and idolized earthly treasures. Those words cut me to the quick. I was broken, and I repented before God.

Several weeks later, the insurance check arrived in the mail for the stolen jewelry. It was within pennies of the amount I knew was needed for the church construction and the amount I had been praying for.

In my brokenness, God showed me I had been praying for others to do what I was not prepared to do myself. I was ashamed it had taken me so many years of my life to truly desire to give back to the Lord. I anonymously donated the insurance check to the church and construction was completed.

> But God knows the delights of our hearts
> and He delights in blessing us.

Over a year after our robbery, I was exhausted physically and mentally and was preparing to leave ministry in any capacity. I prayed to God that if He desired that I continue in any ministry that He give me a sign. I was bold before the Lord! The *next day*, I received a phone call from the police department that a large collection of jewelry had surfaced at a store (two hours away) that bought and sold jewelry. They said there was a possibility some of it might be mine. By then, my case was a closed case with no leads. I accompanied the police to a seedy shop and the owner thrust a piece of jewelry into my hand. He rather brusquely asked, "Is this yours?" I opened my palm and set my eyes upon my gold cross. The police confiscated bags and bags of my jewelry, but much was still missing. I spent the following day at the police station sorting through the jewelry—to catalog it for identification and photographing. Officer after officer stopped in the room and commented how very rare it was that so much would surface a year later in a closed case.

I contacted my insurance company as to how to proceed with repaying the insurance claim. Because there were still pieces missing and so much time had passed, they made the decision to drop any repayment.

The means by which the police knew that (my) jewelry was sold where it was, is that in that particular Pennsylvania county, the stores needed to file a police report every time they purchased jewelry over a certain monetary amount from individuals. Thus, they had the name and address of the young woman who had sold the jewelry. As it turned out, her boyfriend was the perpetrator. He was in jail for another crime at the time. The jewelry was in her home and she sold it. The police questioned both about the remaining missing jewelry, but they were not cooperative.

I would often drive past her home and pray that all would be revealed. Then one day my mother, who was a huge garage sale fan, noticed a garage sale listed at the woman's home. My mother went to the sale and sure enough, there was one of my bracelets she had purchased for me, while on a vacation, which was engraved with my initials. Mom bought the bracelet, and it was the impetus for the police to seek a search warrant. I accompanied them to the house, and they confiscated more bags and bags of my jewelry.

# A Testimony … or a Test of Money

Since then, God has led me to help finance other ministry projects. It seems to always center around jewelry. I sell jewelry pieces to finance ministry and then other pieces of jewelry come back into my life. Strangers will tell me that they were led to give me a piece of jewelry. A goldsmith contacted me and asked if I would work in her shop. Her proposal was that because she was starting out in her business, she had insufficient funds to pay an employee, but would I consider taking my salary in gold jewelry. I did, and the jewelry was even more beautiful than what I had originally owned. I have since sold most of those pieces, as God has directed me, to fund ministry.

Jewelry comes and goes in my life. I still enjoy fine jewelry, but I no longer idolize it. In fact, I delight in God revealing what, where, who, and when He leads me to sell jewelry to fund a ministry project. My story continues, but God's story is ageless.

> As we give to God with a cheerful heart, He will pour out blessings into our lives.

Blessings,

*Becky Bird*

# Fight the Good Fight of Faith

## Danielle Babin

If you have ever found yourself in the middle of a terrifying moment when your faith in God was challenged, you may have found that your faith was strengthened in the turmoil. Is it possible to have peace in the midst of chaos? Yes! Here is an amazing testimony from a successful businesswoman, homeschool mom, minister, and my very dear friend Danielle Babin.

———∞———

This is a word of encouragement to fight the good fight of faith that has real, tangible consequences in the natural. My story starts back in 2006. At the time I was Mom to two girls and two boys under the age of six. The older two girls were in kindergarten and first grade. My husband and I had made the decision to put our oldest girls in public school. I had been a product of both private school and homeschool. I had always considered the public school system to be a scary, brainwashing place where children went to be forever disconnected from their families and the Lord. However, after a series of logical and sheer capacity issues of having two other littles at home, I agreed that the decision to enroll my kids made the most sense.

The night of that decision, I woke up in the middle of the night with a terrible bad panic attack. I have never had one before or since. The heaviness I felt on my chest was real. I felt I couldn't breathe and was going to die. I had no idea what was happening to me. I woke my husband, who happened to be a registered nurse, and he recognized what was happening. I remember lying in bed with tears streaming down my face, crying out to the Lord for relief. In the midst of this, I knew I was terrified of making a decision that would alter my kids' lives. As I cried out in my spirit for relief, I heard the Lord ask me a question. He broke through the pain and asked simply, "Danielle, do you trust me with your kids?" At that moment, it was like I was faced with the truth. I. Did. Not!

I was holding on so tightly to these little gifts I had been given for a moment in time, but I knew they were not mine. They were His. *Do I trust Him?* At that moment, revelation hit me and I surrendered. "Lord, I trust you. You love my kids so much more than I do. I give them to you." At the moment of those words being spoken, it was like a 1,000-pound boulder came off my chest and I could breathe again. The fear was gone instantly. This story is critical to set the stage for the next moment, where the shield of faith was critical for my life.

Now this is where the testimony becomes interesting. Put on your seatbelt. Fast-forward in time nine years, and with the addition of two more kids, we now had two thriving girls and four younger boys. I know some of what I am sharing may seem exaggerated, but I know that we battle not against flesh and blood but against principalities in heavenly places. Ephesians 6:12 says "our struggle is not against flesh and blood, but against the rulers, against the authorities, against the powers of this dark world and against the spiritual forces of evil in the heavenly realms" (NIV).

The natural world reflects the spiritual world. In the middle of the night on December 16, 2016, I woke up from one of those bone-chilling nightmares where, as you wake up, you cannot tell for an instant if it is not truly reality. Fear and pain gripped my heart. I had a nightmare of seeing each of my six kids killed, each in separate, gruesome ways. I gasped for air and could feel a dark presence in my bedroom ... tangible. As I lay in bed, all I could think of was those images in my mind. I felt the heaviness in my room as I lay with my mind racing, and I knew this presence was there to torment me. At that moment, I remembered the battle that had been previously won: the panic attack years before and my surrender to the Lord with each of my kids and trusting Him. I did not audibly say this, but in my spirit, I told the dark, heavy presence: "You need to leave. This has already been settled. The choice has been made and I choose to trust my God to take care of my kids." At that moment, the darkness left the room. Now, these types of spiritual encounters are not common, but I had had several in the past, including angelic encounters. I would normally be shaken by the dream and dark presence as it would make it difficult to sleep, but I fell asleep in the deepest and sweetest sleep ever!

When I woke up the next day, I felt refreshed and did not even feel the effects of the night's battle. I woke up my four sons to get ready for school. It was the typical early morning scramble to get out the door. I remember fussing at Austin, age six, for not preparing his school lunch the night before. As I jumped to start making his lunch, I felt a presence behind me whisper, "Be thankful for every moment." I was instantly reminded of the battle in the night and was immediately hit with thankfulness for my kids.

As we drove down our two-lane Hill Country road to school, it was a drizzly day. I came to a straight section of the highway and saw an oncoming full-sized, double cab pickup truck. He drove onto the shoulder of the road and then jerked the wheel to get back on the road. He proceeded to cross the double yellow lines, heading straight toward our car. I thought, *Oh man, but I can get around him*! I proceeded to turn my vehicle toward

# Fight the Good Fight of Faith

the shoulder to pass him. Impact. I was able to navigate my car enough to where the impact of his truck struck my driver's side, and the brunt force of impact hit the driver's tire, causing it to ram into the cab and pin my leg.

Upon impact, my first thought was, *I knew this was going to happen.* It was like the battle that was fought in the night had prepared me, and the whisper spoken to be thankful for every moment had equipped me. As the truck flipped over our car multiple times and landed on its cab, upside down behind us, I felt the initial impact but then it felt like someone picked up our car because it simply slid to the side of the road so gently.

Multiple screaming ensued from inside our vehicle. The three smaller boys ages six, seven, and nine were in the backseat. Several were yelling in panic. I looked at my son Seth, who was sitting in the front with me. Smoke and smells of airbags and engine filled the car. He looked fine and I proceeded to ask, "Is everyone okay?" Through the noise and panic, I heard "Yes" from all of them. I said, "Thank you, Lord. You are so good, Father!" As I yelled out in thankfulness to the Lord that my sons were all right, I could feel the tangible peace of God. It felt like a cloud of peace filled the car, almost as if you could touch it. It was so tangible! The panic and screaming stopped.

> Rejoice in the Lord always. I will say it again: Rejoice! Let your gentleness be evident to all. The Lord is near. Do not be anxious about anything, but in every situation, by prayer and petition, with thanksgiving, present your requests to God. And the peace of God, which transcends all understanding, will guard your hearts and your minds in Christ Jesus. (Philippians 4:4–7 NIV)

Within seconds, a face appeared by my window. An off-duty fire department officer was heading home from his shift and saw the accident. He asked if I could get out. I looked down at my leg that was crushed by the tire and mangled metal. I knew I had broken ribs on impact and was having difficulty breathing. I could not feel my leg or foot. Our eyes met as he assessed the scene, and I could tell we both thought my leg would have serious injuries. "I can't get you out now, ma'am. I need to get the right equipment, but I will get your kids out now." As the boys exited the car, they looked shaken but appeared to be without injuries.

Upon arrival, the fire department team proceeded to use the "jaws of life" to extract me from the vehicle. It was a slow and intense thirty-five-minute process. As I was loaded into the ambulance, I could see my husband and boys rejoicing in being alive and also praying for me. The other driver was also alive with minor injuries. The assessment was "leg and foot are intact, three broken ribs, lacerated spleen and kidney." I was sent home after one night's stay at the hospital and had multiple days of recovery and therapy.

I received a call from my brother-in-law's sister Ariel, who is an EMT. Upon hearing the names in the accident on the radio, she called the transport team on the scene to see if we were okay. The lead EMT responded, "I think that lady was high on drugs. Someone with that level of trauma should not have been that calm." Ariel's response was, "I know Danielle Babin. She is a pastor's wife and she is not on drugs!"

The truth is the tangible peace of God is beyond human reasoning. The impact of peace that surrounded our car—because we stopped to give thanks in this dark circumstance—allowed others to encounter peace even though they did not recognize it. They reasoned human intervention was the cause of the level of peace that surrounded us. Peace fights against chaos and fear, but it starts with thankfulness.

My prayer in this testimony is for you to have the courage to fight the good fight of faith. Know that we all will encounter our own battles, our "did God really say" moments. Surrendering to who the Lord is *in you and for you* is key. So is knowing you can

# Fight the Good Fight of Faith

trust your Lord to meet you in the darkest moments. Thankfulness in the midst of any circumstance creates tangible and unexplainable peace. You can be prepared for what is ahead, and the Lord is teaching you to be prepared, even if you are not aware. The shield of faith is real to extinguish fiery arrows, and you have access to the full armor of God over your own life.

*Danielle Babin*

Pastor, Shiloh Church
shilohcentral.org

> Therefore, take up the full armor of God, so that you will be able to resist on the evil day, and having done everything, to stand firm. Stand firm therefore, having belted your waist with truth, and having put on the breastplate of righteousness, and having strapped on your feet the preparation of the gospel of peace; in addition to all, taking up the shield of faith with which you will be able to extinguish all the flaming arrows of the evil one. And take the helmet of salvation and the sword of the Spirit, which is the word of God. (Ephesians 6:13–17)

> "Fear not, for I am with you." (Isaiah 43:5 ESV)

# From Death to Life

## (and Back Again)

### Brit Eaton

Life has a way of jerking our emotions around. Sometimes those "bounces" can be brutal, embarrassing, and downright painful. Whether it is a deep emotional trauma or a simple disappointment, there's power in living from the Spirit, a place where our emotions become safe to be transformed in the presence of God. In Christ, we are able to process the tragedies of life in a healthy way, and our lenses become clear to view the things of this realm through the greater reality of the eternal realm. There's no shame in feeling what you feel. God can handle it. And if you lean into Him, even in the midst of heartache, I have no doubt you will find your way to the light, just as my precious friend Brit Eaton—amazing coach, and incredibly talented writer—did.

—∞—

The only thing more complicated than death is resurrection. I never fully understood this pain until I lost my son, *twice*. I was speechless for a season about it, knowing that few could stomach my heart's cry. My laments

## From Death to Life (and Back Again)

too fierce, my despair too real, my grief wasn't exactly "on brand" for my joy-filled, grace-laced communities.

We'd been trying for a year and a half, but I'd told no one. I am not sure why, other than if I couldn't have another child, I did not want to have to admit that I wanted one. Secure in my identity, as I thought I was, I still wanted to be perceived as competent in all aspects of life—even in my family planning.

The unfruitful months went on and on, and I began to make peace with the idea of being a single-child family. Those who are blessed to know my daughter, Bella, understand. She is *so* much more than enough. But she had so much love to give. And so did we. So we kept on in faith, hoping God would not give us a desire He would not fulfill.

And suddenly, there they were. Two little pink lines on a test, like two arms raised high, testifying to God's faithfulness. Still, we told no one. It felt too precious, too new to share. We kept the secret until we couldn't any longer. Roughly twelve weeks in, I knew something was wrong. Symptoms compounded; pain set in. With exactly zero context from my first textbook pregnancy, I built my case with God.

*God, if you choose to take him, I won't fight you.*

*But if you let me raise him, I promise I will love and lead the child straight back to you.*

*I trust you, no matter the outcome.*

*But I'm believing for a miracle.*

I am sure I meant every bit of that surrender. And yet, surrender can be fleeting. The next morning, things got worse. By evening I was en route to the ER. We were forced to tell family, and they rallied quickly to watch Bella while we drove an hour to the hospital in silence. I knew God had taken me at my word and taken my child straight to heaven.

In what felt like a lifetime later, the ER doctor broke the news. "There's a *strong* heartbeat! You and baby are doing just fine!" I burst into tears, startling my care team to concern. They were not used to such joyful responses in their rounds. We were overcome with gratitude, excitement, and sheer awe, and we shared the big news with friends and family. "God brought our baby back from the dead!"

The symptoms subsided and I settled in to rest at home. Three days later, I followed up with my doctor and took my mom along with me. We were bubbling with energy, dreaming and hoping and planning even as we walked into the exam room. We celebrated with my doctor as we shared the ER miracle, and he extended heartfelt and relieved congratulations as he prepped for the ultrasound.

Two seconds into the scan, I sensed a pause in my spirit. The screen quickly confirmed. No wiggling fingers or toes. No signs of little life. Just a tiny silhouette drowning in a uterine black hole. My doctor tried to stay calm, but I could sense the fear in his eyes. He could only muster, "Well ... I'm having a little trouble finding a heartbeat ... but we are going to go down to the 3D room and ..." Everything from that moment on was a nauseating blur.

Kindness, encouragement, and compassion poured from my doctor and his staff, but I couldn't hear a word. Floating along, feeling helpless and hopeless, I caved to the inevitability of my options. A D&C procedure was scheduled for early the next week, but I delivered our son at home the next day.

---

I was so angry with God.

---

A miscarriage was something I knew to be normal, understandable, and ultimately reconcilable. But my heart refused to align with my head. In those dark nights to follow, I began to understand why some people give up on God altogether.

*Is He trustworthy?*

# From Death to Life (and Back Again)

*Is He faithful?*

*Is He really and truly good—in spite of all this evidence to the contrary?*

He gave me no answers but clung to me through fits of rage. And when I collapsed from sheer exhaustion into His arms, He reminded me that death was not what He wanted for me *or* for my child. He sat with me, wept with me, and revealed Himself to me as the Man of Sorrows—acquainted with my grief. He, too, knew what it was like to *bleed out*.

At the end of myself, I dared to ask the question.

*God, did you really give me a miracle? Was it all in my head? What was all that even for?*

He whispered a truth I will never forget.

"Child, even Lazarus died again."

And so we named our son Lazarus.

They say these things get easier with time. I would love to believe that sentiment, but my experience proves otherwise.

> It is not okay. It never was okay. It will never be okay because we were never meant to experience loss in this way.

I lost two more little ones before once again making peace with being a single-child family, and there are days when those losses still sting like new.

And yet, God has made me a spiritual mother to so many—a role I could perhaps not have fulfilled were I busy with my own family. I have learned mothers come in all shapes and sizes, and birthing children is not a prerequisite to embodying the mothering nature and nurture of God.

I still have questions. I still crave answers. But here is what I know for sure.

- My son, Lazarus, was resurrected in mind, body, and spirit in a miracle of God.

- Lazarus lived, even briefly, to remind me God is faithful and in control.
- Lazarus went from death to life—and back again. And in this second death, Lazarus was born to eternal life.

My grief observed? A grace disguised. Thank you, Father.

> "For as in Adam all die, even so in Christ shall all be made alive." (1 Corinthians 15:22 KJV)

## Brit Eaton

Writer, teacher, and spiritual director
www.briteaton.com

# In the Lights of New York City

## Kristin Tucker

We live in the day of influencers. I remember when dreams and aspirations used to be of being mother, nurse, doctor, scientist, or some other world-changing career choice. Today, people often strive to be "influencers." Social media serves up dopamine hit after dopamine hit, keeping us engaged and enveloped in crafty algorithms that keep the likes, shares, and subscribes flowing. Fame is the goal.

We often follow and allow the preferences and approval of others to drive our choices. What an incredible power to have—to influence the choices of others. But honestly, at the heart of it all lies this: most of us just want to be seen and heard.

I dreamed of being famous. I envisioned myself on stage my whole life, but I lacked the confidence to make it happen. I started many things that I never finished, like guitar, piano, dancing, and more. Low self-esteem caused me to quit, but I longed to have confidence. For years, I told my husband, "Don't ever call me onto the platform." I ran from the platform, but slowly, gradually, sometimes painfully, God chiseled away my insecurities.

There are a few in life whose pure confidence has grabbed my attention and kept me in awe. I am talking about confidence with humility and grace carried well. One of those people is my friend Kristin Tucker. She is a powerful singer, life coach, and former stunt woman. She performed in Disney's "Indiana Jones Epic Stunt Spectacular" show for twenty years, jumping off buildings, taking down bad guys, and running through fiery fight scenes. And the fun part is that I saw her perform before I ever met her in person. It has been a privilege to glean from her wisdom and experiences. Here is one moment in her life that will remind you of just how loved you are. No performance necessary.

———∞———

It was late, nearly midnight, and I was so hungry! They had finally let us out of the dance room, where I and fifty other girls had been for the last almost twenty hours. My stomach could be heard roaring over the booming music and the shouts of the choreographer yelling, "Here we go again, 5-6-7-8!"

To be completely honest, at that point I could not have cared less if I was a part of MTV's *Making of the Band* reality show. I had auditioned in Miami and they'd loved me! Now I was in New York City as one of the finalists for the show, and all I wanted was to be invisible. What had started out as such an alluring idea—the possibility of getting picked to be on TV and having my name in "lights"—was turning into a decision I was regretting.

When they finally let us leave for dinner, it was well after midnight. I was starving and was not exactly sure in which direction I was heading. Walking with my head focused on the sidewalk still packed with people, I found myself just a few blocks from Times Square. Although it was past midnight, the lights of the city made it feel much earlier. I had managed to slip out ahead of the rest of the group because I did not want to talk about the big audition the next day with everyone. The

## In the Lights of New York City

truth was, I was actually plotting how I was going to get out of this one.

As I waited to cross the street to grab some food at a deli, I looked up and saw a billboard with an advertisement on it. What struck me was the woman in the picture. She looked like whatever she was selling was the greatest thing she had ever seen. Her face beamed. She was there, for all to see, lit up in the middle of the city that never sleeps. She looked ecstatic, but for whatever reason as I looked up at her in the moment, I felt like I saw past the glitz and caught a glimpse of myself. For the first moment in all of the whirlwind I'd been caught up in, I saw that I was striving to be "famous" because I was so desperate to be seen!

How did I get here?

I had a really good life!

I was a mom to an incredible little boy, who I loved more than anything. I was recently divorced and currently rockin' the divorce diet body (not recommended, but anyone who has gone through one knows it is one of the only perks). I had a great job. I beat up bad guys for a living at the "Indiana Jones Epic Stunt Spectacular" at Disney, and I had a friend group that was amazing. So what was up with this pursuit I was on to be seen? I actually asked myself that very same question before I stepped off the curb and headed to the next block.

Maybe you can relate.

It may not have been your name in lights, but maybe you just wanted some light to shine on you so that you would be noticed. It is crazy. When we do not talk about some of the basic human needs we have for our survival, we can find ourselves pursuing some crazy things just to feel significance. Right?! I mean, my need to be seen was screaming from a basic need to know that I mattered. I was convinced that somehow making the final cut for a reality TV show—that was created to have people see the worst in each other—was going to fulfill a basic need: that maybe I would feel a connection because so many people would see me, get to know my heart, and then love me.

Our basic needs will not go away. If left unattended, we will have them met in worldly ways. There is not a source in the world that will ever be enough to be the one that meets our needs and gives us what we need to be complete.

Which brings me back to that moment. There on the streets of New York, with all the lights and distractions, I felt a prompting from inside. It was so peaceful. It was the voice of my Father, the One who created me and had given me my identity. *You will not find yourself and who you are supposed to be here on the streets of New York City.* He wasn't talking to me about what was to come. He was reminding me that I was loved! Right there, in my mess, I knew my need to be seen would be fulfilled with my eyes on Him. That way I could see the way that He saw me—through His eyes. It was powerful. I was overwhelmed. In that moment, the amount of light I felt shining from within me put the lights of the city to shame. I knew that nothing I was pursuing in the world would light me up the way I was desiring. I let go of what I was pursuing and let His everlasting love for me well up inside me. I literally let myself be loved by the One who is love on the streets of NYC.

This brings me to today. I have spent a lifetime trying to understand love and the desire we all have to obtain it. I have tried at love, and at times had some wins and at other times had some big fails. What I am struck by is that before we can do anything at all in love, we have to allow ourselves to be loved. It is interesting because I think a lot of us, me included, attempt to go out and give away what we do not feel in full possession of yet, secretly desiring to be loved in return. It is normal, it is one of our basic needs.

But …

# In the Lights of New York City

What changes everything is the time spent allowing ourselves to be loved by our Creator, letting Him love us in the middle of our messes, right where we do not even like ourselves. I know it changed everything for me.

> I realized that until I allowed my source of love to come from the fountain that will never run dry, Jesus, I was going to continue to tap into sources that would leave me dry.

Our source for all needs is the One who created us, and He is the only way to really achieve that feeling of being complete. From that place of understanding our value, we can then go and live loved! We are not trying to get it in what we do or what others think of us. We are living it every day from the overflow of Him first loving us.

What about you?

Have you given yourself permission to live loved?

I would love to hear from you about how you live loved too.

*Kristin Tucker*

Website: https://www.kristintucker.me
Facebook: /Kristin.SacredGarden
Instagram: kristuckspecialk

# But I'm Right!

### Eve Passmore

Oh, the amount of noise and number of voices, debates, and opinions we muddle through from day to day! It never seems to end, and it rarely seems that people are teachable. Instead, they are sure they are right. Unfortunately, this epidemic exists even within the church. Perhaps you've found yourself floating in the muck of verbal assaults and battles that some justify as being "iron sharpening iron." God forgive us for misusing that Proverbs 27:17 scripture.

If your heart has ached over religious debates, philosophies, and ideologies, there's beauty in simply falling into the arms of Jesus, who is grace Himself. In my eyes, my dear friend Eve Passmore is grace, just like Christ. She is a rare jewel on this earth. Even nature responds to her in a way that prompts me to refer to her as "Mother Nature," and I am sure it is because of the grace-filled nurture she carries everywhere she goes. Eve so eloquently expresses what God showed her about people's need to be right and where that landed her.

―∞―

## The Backstory

Scrolling quickly through my newsfeed, I stumbled across a post recently put up by an excited young friend who had just participated in an interdenominational "unity" event among local churches. Something along the lines of:

# But I'm Right!

"Praise the Lord! The church is coming together to worship beyond denominational divides! Walls are coming down!

"God is so good!"

Something we can all celebrate, right? Yeah ... not so much. Sadly (but not surprisingly) fellow evangelicals saw the post and jumped on the opportunity to dive in for the needed "pick apart." So it began.

"My brother, this is wrong because ..."

"Christians shouldn't ..."

"But, my friend, the Bible says ..."

"*We* are ___, but *they* are ___, and therefore we need to keep our distance ..."

And before I knew it, there we were, all definitively chopped back up into little denominational, doctrinal pieces all over his Facebook wall. The Catholics over there, the Baptists over here; the charismatics, Pentecostals, and even "greasy gracers" all finding their tiny, safe fan clubs and echo chambers among the would-be theologians and armchair pastors compelled to join the conversation! To be fair, this one did not get as heated as some I have seen; there was definitely some restraint practiced. I even saw a line in there about loving all (of those in error, from a safe distance)!

But I have to say, it felt a bit hollow. So I was sad.

Sad for the naive young fellow who thought a unity celebration was a *good* thing and got the riot act read publicly to him on his own wall (by those declaring themselves to be more knowledgeable about unity).

Sad for those engaging in the debate with that heart-pounding need to strike a blow that could not be returned. I know that feeling; I have been there.

Sad for those who were being cut, once again, from the "in" group and sent back to "out," where they are loved and prayed for but are not to be trusted.

Sad for those reading who were now left in the position of judge. *Who is right? What of those who get it wrong?*

But as I let that sadness roll around in my heart a little bit, I realized there was something else growing in there too. The sense of injustice, frustration, and sadness, while not being rushed out the door, was gradually being replaced by ... what was it? Appreciation?

Wonder and gratitude began to well up in me as I realized: *I don't feel any sense of urgency to fix this! I don't feel the need to defend my perspective of God tooth and nail. I no longer have to fight to be right as if my life depended on it.* Because here is the kicker: I no longer believe that it does.

I no longer live in fear of my current religious belief being wrong. (I am actually pretty confident that it *is* wrong! I have probably got more wrong about Him than I have got right.) But He's got me so convinced of His love for me that I am no longer scared He is going to burn me alive for the stuff I misunderstand. It is kinda nice, I gotta say.

I actually have confidence that His Holy Spirit can lead me into all truth and that I don't have to fear "missing it." I have come to the conclusion that His:

*love is bigger than my ability to comprehend it.

*truth is larger than my capacity for it.

*grace is greater than my grasp of it.

So, yeah. While I am still kinda bummed about the way that wall post about walls coming down caused a bunch more walls to be thrown up, I am also thankful. I am thankful for conversations that challenge. For passions that flare. For views that differ. For the many, many others who value the Author of

## But I'm Right!

Truth more than their version of His words. For those who love loving even more than they love being right. And I am so glad to have a God whose rightness and goodness trump my wrongness forever.

—∞—

Speaking in tongues is not the point; love is. It is neither angelic eloquence, nor the mastery of human language that persuades. It does not matter how poetic, prophetic, or profound I may sound; my conversation is reduced to the hollow noise of clanging brass cymbals if loves echo is absent.

I could predict the future in detail and have a word of knowledge for everyone. I could possess amazing faith, and prove it by moving mountains! It does not make me any more important than anyone else. Love is who you are! You are not defined by your gift or deeds.

Love is not about defending a point of view; even if I am prepared to give away everything I have and die a martyr's death; love does not have to prove itself by acts of supreme devotion or self-sacrifice! Love is large in being passionate about life and relentlessly patient in bearing the offenses and injuries of others with kindness. Love is completely content and strives for nothing. Love has no desire to make others feel inferior and has no need to sing its own praises.

Love is predictable and does not behave out of character. Love is not ambitious. Love is not spiteful and gets no mileage out of another's mistakes. Love sees no joy in injustice. Loves delight is in everything that truth celebrates.

Love is a fortress where everyone feels protected rather than exposed! Loves persuasion is persistent! Love believes. Love never loses hope and always remains constant in contradiction.

Love never loses its altitude! Prophecies will cease. Tongues will pause. The quest for knowledge will be inappropriate when perfection is grasped.

What we perceived in prophetic glimpses is now concluded in completeness!

When I was an infant I spoke infant gibberish with the mind of an infant; my reasoning also was typical of an infant; how it all changed when I became a man! I am an infant no more!

There was a time of suspense, when everything we saw was merely mirrored in the prophetic word, like in an enigma; but then I gaze face-to-face; behold, I am in him! Now I may know even as I have always been known!

Now persuasion and every pleasurable expectation is completed in agape. Agape is the superlative of everything faith and hope always knew to be true about me! Love defines my eternal moment! (1 Corinthians 13 Mirror Bible)

*Eve Passmore*

Owner of Eden Abbey Brewing
www.edenabbeybrewing.com

# Sitting in Sadness

### Tiffany Matthews

I am honored to call my friend Tiffany Matthews to the table. She is an incredible wife, mother, singer, worship leader, and senior leader at The Gate in Charlotte, North Carolina. I have had the privilege of knowing Tiffany for several years, and I have seen her navigate some of the most painful, challenging situations with grace. If you were to see the smile on her face and the joy she exudes while worshipping on the platform and while serving others, you probably wouldn't suspect that she's known deep loss. Here is a woman who has learned the power of sitting in sadness with Jesus by her side.

—∞—

It was the official start to the Christmas season, the season where my life blood comes alive! On top of that, our church had been experiencing revival and outpouring for just over a year and had decided, by the Lord's leading, that we were to take the month of December to rest. I had so much overflowing goodness, excitement, expectation, giddiness, and holiday cheer just oozing out of me while coming into that month of rest. Not only did I finally get to pull out all the stops for Christmas once again, but I also had more time to celebrate since the church calendar was stripped bare.

I started strong and jolly by saying yes to all the Christmas parties and Christmas activities, dragging my family to every event that even remotely smelled like Christmas. It was time to live large and make all the memories. As the month went on, I never slowed down, but I began to notice that I was not basking in joy during all of these moments. I was starting to go through the motions of painting on a smile and doing the holly jolly things, but I was actually feeling more and more disconnected and empty as the month went on. My husband began to question me, question all of my activities along the way, and ask if I was okay or if I needed to slow down. I was determined that I just needed some more Christmas cheer and could muscle my way all through Christmas. And that's just what I did.

Yet the day after Christmas, the bottom came out and I tailspun into a crash-and-burn. I could hardly get out of bed, and it felt like the whole month and Christmas itself were meaningless. It was honestly terrifying to see how fast my world crumbled. I sat with my husband, who gave me a safe place to outwardly process my month. In the end, I realized I had too much sadness in my heart. I was drowning in grief. That's when it hit me: I lost my father and my brother to tragic deaths and both of their birthdays were in December. Not only that, but my epiphany also came exactly on my brother's birthday, the day after Christmas. My body was grieving and I had completely disconnected my heart from it all. For years I had been on a journey of healing and releasing my emotions, and I realized right then that I had never properly grieved my brother and father. I had just pushed down the sadness because it felt too big and it made me feel too small. In doing that, though, I could hardly think about them, remember them, or celebrate them on their special days. To forget the sadness and grief, I had practically forgotten about them! In that month, my heart was saying "No more!" My husband and I spent the day in tenderness and sadness, connecting the dots of my internal world. It felt very comforting to know that all my "crazy" made sense.

I even thought I was done and had made big progress as I headed into our staff meeting the following week. I had so much revelation and understanding. Yet, as they were beginning to talk about starting back up our schedule of services, prayer meetings, discipleship classes, etcetera, etcetera, etcetera, I felt like I couldn't get out of the room quickly enough. Our normal schedule felt like death to me. That is when I knew that revelation did not equal healing, and the time had come to make a decision. In actuality, I was still drowning in my big, newfound emotions, so my husband stepped in and laid the table for me, so to speak.

He rented a small cabin on Prayer Mountain in Moravian Falls for me to be completely alone for almost a week. He told me that he would set up everything if I would just be brave enough to go. As I packed my bag, I realized that this was the first time in my adult life to go somewhere alone. We had gotten married and had kids at a very young age, and we did everything together. Now, being almost forty, I was heading off alone for the first time, and in me was a big, jumbled ball of exhilaration and terror. I had no one to rely on and no one to distract me; it was just me, my heart, and God.

I did it! I got in my rental car and made it to my little cabin. I even started my own little woodburning stove. I never stepped foot outside the cabin for those four days. I ended up spending every morning weeping about the injustice of losing two of the closest men in my life. I would vacillate between being angry at God, being angry at them, and being angry with myself for all of the missed moments when they were alive, and after they had gone. I journaled and journaled and journaled every thought and every emotion. What I witnessed and experienced was that with every hurt I opened up and let the mess out of—even if it was chewing God out or asking Him if He really was good to take so much life—comfort would find me in the end; it always found me in the end. I finally felt truthful, authentic, and real. I realized that I had picked up an orphan spirit and identified as being fatherless.

As I learned to sit in my sadness—to own it, feel it, and explore it—I was able to connect my heart again to my earthly father, which led to connecting my heart to my heavenly Father. Then I was able to receive comfort and that "peace that surpasses understanding." Now I am able to integrate grief into myself as being a part of my story. It is not something I have to minimize to look strong. It does not take away my ability to have faith or to believe in the miraculous for others when I did not get my own. I learned that it was actually the *fear* of grieving that was depriving me of comfort and solace.

After that trip with me, my heart, and I, I have noticed that I am able to think of my father and brother more regularly. I can reminisce with my family and let them still have a space in my life. Most of all, I can now tap into the goodness I had in those connections and relationships. I can think of them and smile, and my heart is flooded with the joy of having known them and lived with them and created memories with them.

> The gift of grief is the restoration of joy and the restoration of life.

The very thing that I was running from for years was the very key to opening the door to healing and connection, to being able to actually see the life I *have* instead of the life I lost.

Do not fear grief and sadness, they are the gifts you need to keep living.

*Tiffany Matthews*

Senior Leader
The Gate, Charlotte, North Carolina
www.wearethegate.com

# Freedom from Panic Attacks

## Jeanne Kaufman

One dear woman in my life has been an inspiration for rising above anxiety. If you have ever found yourself muddling through the darkness of fear and anxiety, you will know the impact of overcoming such an enemy. Jeanne Kaufman is like a walking, shimmering light on this earth. If you met her, you would never know that she had come through the darkness of mental turmoil because she radiates faith and joy in a profoundly beautiful way. The woman you are about to hear from now travels all over the world, ministering to the poorest of the poor and sharing the message of Jesus fearlessly. Jeanne is a true inspiration!

—∞—

I love the word "calm." It is a state of mind that I treasure. I also love that Jesus promised He will *keep us* in 'perfect peace' when *we keep* our minds on Him. "You will keep in perfect peace all who trust in you, all whose thoughts are fixed on you!" (Isaiah 26:3 NLT). He keeps when we keep! It is my prayer, as I testify of being healed of mental torment, that you also will experience the perfect peace Jesus provides. His plan for us on this earth is to walk in peace always. "Now may the Lord of peace himself give you peace at all times and in every way. The Lord be with all of you" (2 Thessalonians 3:16 NIV).

My story begins one morning in April of 1997. I woke up a little dizzy with a headache and immediately started to feel nervous about it. Negative thoughts ensued, causing me to emotionally spiral downward. An unreasonable fear came on me with the ridiculous concern of *I am no longer a Christian*. This was terribly disturbing and I felt chilled to the bone. I prayed in desperation, quoting, "[I] will not be afraid of evil tidings: [my] heart is steadfast, trusting in the LORD" (Psalm 112:7 NKJV).

I spoke the name of Jesus out loud, then attempted to go about my daily activities. Spiritually, I had opened a door to demonic attack. Struggles continued. Another intrusive thought came, catching me completely off guard. It is important to mention that the terrifying thought was *not* my own thought. The foreign impression was as brief as it was devastating. I did not know it was the voice of a demon whispering to me, "Jesus isn't real." I staggered in shock. I thought it was *my* thought, but it was the voice of a "stranger" (John 10:5). I felt so vulnerable, scared, and unstable.

After medical tests, I found there was nothing physically wrong with me. It was a spiritual battle. The enemy had gained an entrance into my mind for several months. I was caught off guard and had been broadsided. This dreadful combination of symptoms seemed unbearable for me to handle.

Daniel 7:25 (paraphrased) says, "Satan comes to wear out the saints." I was worn out physically, mentally, and spiritually. As I searched the Scriptures diligently for healing and peace, I began to find answers for every problem I was facing. In those dark moments, I felt like the disciples in John 6:68 saying, "Lord, to whom shall we go? You [alone] have the words of eternal life" (AMP). I knew He alone was my hope for healing. The following verses became a source of strength and comfort for me:

1. **Sudden Fear.** Proverbs 3:25 – "Do not be afraid of sudden fear (panic) nor of the onslaught (attack) of the wicked when

it comes" (NASB1995, parentheticals mine). "Be not afraid of sudden fear" was God's personal instruction on how to handle a panic attack. Instead of focusing on being afraid of "sudden fear," I learned to recognize the pattern in these mental attacks and how to not give them any power.

2. **Power over the Enemy.** Luke 10:19 – "Behold, I give unto you power to tread on serpents and scorpions, and over *all* the power of the enemy: and nothing shall by any means hurt you" (KJV). When my thoughts began to spin and I was feeling fear, I learned to call on Jesus's name.

> Without fail, a calming peace would fill my racing mind, my heart, and my body.

I read this many times saying, "Nothing will hurt me." Rehearsing thoughts laced with fear resulted in turmoil and loss of peace. The enemy here can get a hold, or as the Bible says, a "stronghold," in our mind. Learn to take every thought captive (2 Corinthians 10:3–5).

3. **Trust Jesus.** 1 Peter 5:7 – "Cast all your anxiety on Him, because He cares about you." I did not know what to do. I needed help! There were times I had to totally throw myself over to the Lord for His keeping. I mentally rehearsed *He will take care of me.*

4. **Believe in Truth.** John 14:6 – "Jesus said to him, 'I am the way, the truth, and the life'" (NKJV). John 10:10: "I came so that they would have life, and have it abundantly." Daily, I saturated myself with truths from the Bible to learn to discern the truth from lies. I confessed God's Word that my future was bright according to Jeremiah 29:11: "For I know the thoughts that I think toward you, says the Lord, thoughts of peace and not of evil, to give you a future and a hope" (NJKV). I replaced thoughts of hopelessness with hope from verses like this.

5. **Comforted with Jesus's Love.** Hebrews 13:5 – Jesus said, "'I will never leave you nor forsake you'" (NKJV). Daily I confided in the Holy Spirit and developed an intimate friendship with Him, growing in confidence of His presence with me through all my emotions.

6. **Journal What God Says.** Habakkuk 2:2 – "Then the LORD answered me and said: 'Write the vision and make it plain on tablets, that he may run who reads it'" (NKJV). Write the truth down on paper. There is power in the written word. Seeing the words that you have written on paper adds a strong visual sense. This helped immensely to remind me of His promises.

7. **New Beginnings.** Romans 12:2 – "Be transformed by the renewing of your mind" (NKJV). The recurring thought I had wrestled with, *I wish I was normal; I wish I was normal,* is now a thing of the past. Refusing to listen to the wrong voice is a decision I made. I have been made new in the spirit of my mind and have put on the "new man." My mind has been healed. I now have the mind of Christ. I have never known such peace as I do now. Troubled thoughts, anxieties, panic attacks, and near insanity are completely gone. I met the Prince of Peace! His name is Jesus. My prayer for you is that love will override any fear that has taken root in your soul.

8. **Let Peace Rule.** Colossians 3:15–16 – "Let the peace of Christ [the inner calm of one who walks daily with Him] be the controlling factor in your hearts [deciding and settling questions that arise]. To this peace indeed you were called as members in one body [of believers]. And be thankful [to God always]. Let the [spoken] word of Christ have its home within you [dwelling in your heart and mind—permeating every aspect of your being]" (AMP).

9. **Your Own Personal Counselor.** Isaiah 9:6 – "To us a child is born, to us a son is given; and his name shall be called

Wonderful Counselor, Mighty God, Everlasting Father, Prince of Peace" (ESV). I used to long for a counselor who could help me and advise me. In Scripture I discovered we have our own guidance counselor through the Holy Spirit.

My closing prayer: May the secure tranquility that comes through Jesus's love fully envelop you and bring you lasting assurance, with peace in your heart and mind. Amen.

*Pastor Jeanne Kaufman*

The Tabernacle, Brookings, South Dakota
www.holylifetabernacle.com

# God Sent a Bus!

### Bonnie Goolsby

Have you ever found yourself in a difficult situation that is topped with other difficulties, or layer after layer of obstacles? When you are in those situations, it can be hard to stay in a place of peace, especially where sickness abounds. When your body does not feel right, it seems harder to keep your mind and emotions feeling right. That's why this story from my sweet friend Bonnie Goolsby is inspirational. Her experience testifies that no matter where you are in this world and no matter the circumstances, God makes a way. Her faith in God is what makes her so powerful as a leader who influences other leaders. I am blessed to know Bonnie.

---

January of 2021 will forever be etched in my mind. My husband, Ray, and I traveled to Ireland for the birth of a grandson. It was a tumultuous time for the nations, including navigating COVID-19 restrictions while traveling. Our trip was no exception.

The night before we were to fly to Ireland, the US government released a notification that travel back into the States by a certain date would require a negative COVID test. Because we had personally dealt with COVID at the end of the 2020 holiday season, we knew we would show positive if given a COVID test. Ray immediately went online and changed our return date so we would reenter the States prior to the new policy going into action.

# God Sent a Bus

Fast-forward a few weeks and it was time for us to return to the States. Our flight was early in the day, and we had to travel from Northern Ireland to Dublin Airport—in the Republic of Ireland. Normal travel time would have been three and a half hours. Our son-in-law drove us in his mother's car because it was big enough to handle us and all our luggage. By 6:00 a.m. we were on the road. The temperature was frigid, and ice was on the car. About an hour into the trip, snow began to fall heavily. The sight was breathtaking and was pretty much a whiteout situation. I rested my head and closed my eyes. In a moment's time, I felt the car begin to go out of control. We were hydroplaning. Due to leaving so early in the morning, the roads had not been gritted yet. I sat up immediately and thought we were about to hit the side of a semi, or as referred to in Ireland, a lorry. All I had time to do was scream "Jesus." He was there. We slid through two oncoming lanes of traffic and hit the wall of an overpass. My son-in-law quickly tried to restart the car and moved us to the opposite side of the road.

The three of us were stunned! Crazily enough, we did not even ask each other how we were doing. The car was totaled. My son-in-law was concerned about the insurance coverage since he was driving his mother's car. Funny thing—I'd happened to have a random conversation with his mom the day before and she'd told me that she had kept David on her insurance. I was able to console my son-in-law with that information.

> Sounds like God to me! He is very much into the details of our lives.

As Ray and my son-in-law exited the car to survey the damage, my son-in-law saw a bus pull up to the exit behind us. It was headed in the opposite direction but had come to a stop. My son-in-law ran over to the bus and spoke with the driver.

Before we knew it, the bus had pulled around and pulled up directly next to us. It was headed to Dublin Airport!

I was concerned about paying the driver because we did not have the proper currency. My son-in-law said not to worry, that the driver would not charge us. I wasn't sure if he was assuming that or knew that. Our luggage was promptly loaded into the luggage bay, and Ray and I stepped up into the bus cab. As we walked past the shielded plexiglass box designed to protect the driver from COVID, I caught his gentle and caring glance. Our eyes did the talking. Ray and I were masked for COVID and still stunned by the accident.

Ray and I took our seats but did not talk to each other for at least another forty-five minutes. The shock of everything happening so quickly had quieted us, and we were in that head and heart space of sitting with the Lord. Ray was the first to speak up, and he asked how I was doing. We had both experienced some minor injuries but were otherwise doing okay. We called our son-in-law, and it was the same for him. A lorry had pulled up under the overpass to wait out the snowstorm, and my son-in-law was able to sit in his truck to wait for the tow truck to arrive. Thank you, Lord! He was able to stay warm during the wait.

Ray and I never fretted over whether we would make our flight in time. God had sent a bus! A bus going to Dublin Airport! It was not just a city bus. It was deluxe! We traveled for over two hours. As we were exiting the bus at the airport terminal, the driver smiled at us and did not charge us. A glance of heartfelt gratitude was given. We arrived at our gate with ten minutes of boarding time left. That was enough time to get a coffee. Can you say amen?!

I spent the flight underneath my shawl weeping with thanks to the Lord. He is so good! He was with us the entire time. We were all safe, and God had sent a deluxe bus headed to the airport from two hours away. The lorry came just in time for my son-in-law to get out of the cold and have a warm place to wait for the tow truck.

My son-in-law's mother got another car with her insurance. I had told her the Lord was going to give her another car with all the bells and whistles. She did not know what that meant, as it is not an Irish term. The car dealer told her he had a car for her with all the bells and whistles. God is so fun!

So, when facing challenging situations these days, I remind myself that God sent a bus. The Lord asked Ray to interpret what had happened. Vehicles represent ministry. It was a word for us concerning the ministry God was leading us into. You see, it was not just a bus. It was a deluxe bus! Doors are opening for ministry that we never thought were possible.

*Bonnie Goolsby*

www.raygoolsby.com

# I Choose Him

### Jennifer Hart Shaw

Have you stopped to consider the choices you make on a daily basis? There's more power in your choices than you can imagine. Being yielded to the Holy Spirit and giving God your consistent yes is what leads to powerful, beautiful bonds of covenant that are designed to grow and bless your life and lives around you. Even when the choice to say yes is challenging, it is always worth it. My dear friend Jennifer Hart Shaw shares her thoughts that serve as a reminder that we have solid ground when we align our desires with God's way, and when we don't feel the desire, our yes to Him transforms our desires.

—∞—

Life is filled with choices. Some are easy, like which detergent to buy or what restaurant to eat at. Some are harder, like choosing a church, a career, or a place to live. Even more difficult and with more consequence comes choosing a spouse or committing to a faith.

I think back to a time in my life when I had a big choice to make, a choice that would affect the rest of my life. I had to choose whether I was going to marry my boyfriend. Isn't it amazing to be asked that one big question? A question my boyfriend had already thought about, prayed about, and decided. But if you are the one getting proposed to, you might not have done all the thinking and praying and decision-making before getting asked. What pressure to give an immediate answer! Although, if I am honest, most women are doing the thinking long before that proposal comes.

# I Choose Him

In my case, I had already made the decision that I would say yes if asked (way before I actually got proposed to). It was not an easy choice though. I really did struggle with it for a bit, unsure if he was *the one*. Ultimately, I chose my husband. And I have continued to choose him every day since. We have been married for almost thirty years, and every day we are together is a reflection not only of the choice we made at the altar, but also of the choices we make daily: the choice to *choose* each other and to honor, love, and respect one another. We are not happily married because we are lucky. We are happily married because of the thousands of choices we have made to not mess it up.

It reminds me of my walk with God. A good relationship with a divine Creator I cannot see or audibly hear does not happen accidentally. It requires some effort. Much like my marriage, it requires that I choose Jesus. Every. Day. I choose to follow His leading, walk in His ways, and reflect His nature. I cannot possibly know where He leads, what direction He walks in, nor understand His ways unless I spend time with Him through worship, prayer, and studying the Bible. And to take it a step further, I cannot truly live out my faith unless I allow it to be tested by being in fellowship with other people. The same goes for my marriage. It is the testing in our lives that has bonded us deeply and made our relationship the most special and unique human relationship that we have.

In John 6, we read that Jesus had been ministering to the multitudes with His disciples. There was a time when even His own disciples were questioning Him. His words did not make sense to them, and He contradicted their religious beliefs. He really offended them when He said, "'Unless you eat the flesh of the Son of Man and drink His blood, you have no life in you'" (John 6:53 NKJV). After this, many of His disciples left Him. They just could not continue to follow Him when He was not making sense to them. Jesus asked the Twelve, "'Do you also want to go away?'" (v. 67). Simon Peter answered Him, "'Lord, to whom shall we go? You have the words of eternal life'" (v. 68).

This passage sticks with me and has helped to define my faith over the years.

> Following Christ does not always make sense and it is not always easy. In fact, oftentimes it would seem to be a lot easier to *not* follow Christ.

Our flesh and the pressure from the world certainly tempt us to turn away every single day. But here, Simon Peter basically said there was nowhere and no one else they could turn to because only Jesus has the words of eternal life. In other words, nothing else mattered.

We choose You, Lord. Even when it does not make sense and You sound a little crazy. Even when it costs us something and we have to leave all that we know behind. Even when we are being persecuted and we may lose our life. We choose *You.*

Much like the commitment I made to my husband, I have also made this commitment to God, and I am convinced there is nothing that would cause me to walk away from Him. I don't have to understand or even like everything He does. I chose Him and I do it again and again.

I often say that the good things of God require a sacrifice. By choosing to follow God no matter what, I give up my choice to walk away. I can do that, knowing that He is good, He is faithful, and He loves me.

*Jennifer Hart Shaw*

Senior Leader

# The Unbeatable Power

## Kayla Roberts

Have you ever looked in the face of violence? Have you ever wondered what is going on in the hearts of offenders? It is easy for us to see the evil behind the violence, but are we able to look beyond the facade to find the truth about someone's destiny, even when they put the devil on display? I have been challenged in the best way by my dear friend Kayla Roberts, as she's worked with some of the most impossible (even demonically possessed people, I might add) in her line of work. Her testimony will leave you pondering the power of God and immense love.

―∞―

My testimony of this event that took place in my counseling practice is definitely something I had not signed up for. In the movie *The Silence of the Lambs*, released back in the early '90s, there is a young FBI agent named Clarice who was utterly intimidated by a psychopath asking her "Are you scared, Clarice?" Well, I found myself in Clarice's shoes one day in my office when greeted with the utmost intimidation of a classic criminal mind. He came to me for counseling, describing his rage and predatorial behaviors, letting me know that it turned him on when he inflicted pain and suffering on others. He liked intimidating other people.

Violence was his default position in life and thus he proudly asserted his strength as a man. He longed to feel powerful that way. His heroes were a number of other criminals and psychopaths. He had a record of domestic violence and typically beat his partners, not to mention made typical threats to other people, as he liked to "screw with people's minds," to put it in his words.

He came to me for counseling because he was afraid that one day he would end up in jail. His own rage began to scare him, although it had become his identity.

> When I encountered this case, I thought to myself: *I did not sign up for this.*

Then I began to get upset with God for letting that happen, and with myself for not screening my cases better so that I did not end up in predicaments like this where my own safety was at risk.

After explaining his violence, he asked me, "Are you scared?" Then I heard myself saying: "Not at all. That is not impressive to me." He leaned in with interest, surprise, and curiosity as I began to tell him about having power with God and how love trumps any other force on the face of this planet.

"Love gives you unbeatable power!" I said to a power-thirsty criminal mind. I had his attention as I began to introduce him to a God very different from what he had learned from his Christian upbringing. Needless to say, he had warned me to not talk about God because he was not interested. But as he kept talking about hate, I counteracted it with mercy and love in the ultimate expression of God's grace—to love humanity in a radically crazy way. The icing on the cake was when I told him he was loved that way and that his sins were forgiven! He was dumbfounded.

# The Unbeatable Power

His violence and bloodthirsty acts were not sufficient to convince me that God had given up on loving him. The contrary was true. God was in fact drawn to loving on him all the more, despite his own resistance toward God. Where sin abounds, love abounds even more! I gave him example after example of what God's love looked like, all the while refusing to judge him for his violent acts. I began to lean in to his experience with compassion, empathizing with him for the agony of his own rage.

He finally asked me, "What church do you go to? My family are all Christians and I grew up going to church, but I have never heard about a God that sounds like yours." As the months went by, he tested my love for him. He confessed many of his sins and my response never changed. I told him that I forgave him and so did God (John 20:23). His eyes started to light up with a newfound beaming hope!

He made mistakes and then told me about them, and I kept giving him hope that God's love for him did not change and that God did not leave him. His behavior started to change. He stopped his violent acts. He reconciled with his partner—previously a foreign concept for him. He called on Jesus in my office and turned his life over to God. He finally found what he had longed for all his life. After he stopped coming to counseling, I was afraid he might have turned his back on God again, until he wrote a year later. He let me know how he had turned his life around since he had stepped foot in my counseling room, and that he was never the same. He was so grateful for the life he had found in Jesus!

As it turned out, I had stepped into a big pile of mess with this case, and my tempting thoughts were that this was a lost cause, though I did not admit that out loud, and then love won! It always does. All I had to do was partner with love and let Jesus do the rest. The client did not even have a need to continue seeing me for the miracle to continue to take place in his life. That seed of God's love inside him germinated into a whole new tree, full of life.

## Kayla Roberts

Licensed Mental Health Counselor
Senior Leader, Encounters Church
www.encounterschurch.com

# The Redemptive Work

## in the Midst of Trauma

### Katie Thorpe

Have you ever "met" someone via social media who became dear to your heart? Many years ago, I received a personal message on Facebook from a dear woman who reached out after reading one of my posts about my desire to have outdoor worship gatherings that were not the norm—in barns, fields, and such. Worshiping in the elements where I can feel the wind and see God's handiwork in motion seems to be an easy way to connect with the One who made it all. I often think it is odd that we call people to worship the Creator of the entire universe in manmade boxes where we cannot see His art (except for each other, of course). It sounds silly when you think about it. "We'll build this container and You can meet us there, Lord." Honestly, though, I understand the need for gathering spaces that keep us cool in the heat and warm in the winter. I get it!

Back to the messenger: the woman who messaged me seemed to completely understand my heart for meeting in unusual places. She also understood my childlike heart. On top of that, when Bill and I were sick, she sent us food before I'd even had the chance to meet her in person. Katie Thorpe is like a fairy godmother who makes life magical and sweet, even from a distance. I am so thankful for this dear friend who has been a blessing at every turn. She glows, literally glows, with joy and radiance. Her strength in the face of difficult circumstances is one that refuses to stay in the darkness. She will always choose joy and childlike belief no matter what is happening around her. I have come to greatly admire Katie, and I know her words will bless you. I pray you can feel the radiant, childlike trust that inspired her words.

———∞———

There is only one way a broken life can be completely healed and restored and that is through the redemptive work of Jesus Christ. If you are alive on this planet for any amount of time, you will experience pain—physical, emotional, or mental. This usually results in trauma, but not at God's hands, like so many believe. But not everyone knows there is access to His healing to move on from the pain. I think most people think of healing as physical, but emotional and mental healing are just as important to God. For me, the words in Isaiah 53, "Surely he took up our pain and bore our suffering" (Isaiah 53:4 NIV) became so real that it has become my heart to see people healed from trauma.

There is a passage in Psalm 94 that I believe shows even deeper how much Jesus took this pain for us. "I restored that which I took not away (Psalm 69:4 KJV).

> Trauma steals from us, but Jesus is standing with arms wide open, and there is healing in His hands.

If you have ever seen God as the One who has caused harm, take a close look at Jeremiah 29:11. He has a plan that He declares over you, a plan to prosper you and *not* to harm you, to

# The Redemptive Work in the Midst of Trauma

give you *hope* and a *future*. If you have experienced the opposite so far in your life, I am here today to give you *hope*.

I have been through my share of trauma—religious trauma that showed God as anything but a loving father. I suffered severe depression and anxiety for three years after a very difficult and traumatic pregnancy in 2015, then both of my parents died of cancer two years apart—my dad in 2017 and my mom in 2019. But something really unusual happened after my mom died. God showed up in the most miraculous way. Something that could have plunged me deeper into depression became the catalyst for bringing me freedom. And no, my mom dying of cancer was not God's plan, but He did use it in the most beautiful way to bring grace into my life.

Grace is the most beautiful thing I have ever experienced. Grace is Jesus and all that He did on the cross to bring us into complete wholeness. I don't think I had ever truly seen that His death and resurrection were my freedom. Learning to receive His abundance of grace changed my life so drastically that people began to comment on my appearance. I believe people saw a manifestation of God's glory. Healing was beautiful for me. I was broken but He restored me. I love to talk about restoration and redemption. It is the joy of my heart to share with others and see them transformed by the grace of God.

If you are walking in pain today from trauma, I am praying for a complete restoration for you and for every broken place to be restored and redeemed.

Grace and peace to you,

*Katie Thorpe*

# God's Plan A

## Hannah Wakeman

Have you ever felt demeaned, belittled, or left behind simply because you are a woman? Women have known centuries of oppression, some even being seen as valueless as a dog. We have come a long way, but there's still a remnant of that small thinking that lingers today. And would you believe it is still in the church, despite the fact that God chose to make His entrance into this world through a woman? I admire ladies who have not shrunk back into the darkness but have stepped out into the calling God has placed on their lives. I am thankful to know many of these powerhouses. My friend Hannah Wakeman is one of many who remembered that she was God's "Plan A." Read the story of this amazing lady.

―∞―

When was the moment you realized you could walk in who God created you to be? The time you realized it wasn't just a daydream or wishful thinking? Maybe that moment is happening now as you read this encouraging book. You can say to yourself that you are enough or that your giftings can change the world, and you can even hear it being told to you, but it is another thing to actually take a step of faith into the God-given calling on your life. This is especially challenging when you don't see other women model it for you.

In my early twenties, I was on the pastoral team at my church. My senior pastor was planning to retire, and one of the other key associate pastors had left ministry tragically. He had been a role model, and I had assumed we would be working

## God's Plan A

together in the future. I found myself feeling betrayed, disoriented, and lost. *If he isn't pastoring on my team with the support he has been providing, how can I walk in my calling?* This question was hidden until I realized my confidence had been pulled out from under me when he left. It is easy to preach it, teach it, or counsel it, but every one of us has to actually face the question: Do I believe that God has made me enough for what I am called to do? Do I really believe I can walk in God's Plan A for my life?

Let's just laugh at the setup—I was the youngest leader on our pastoral team at age twenty-five, single, and a woman. Now, depending on where you are from, that might not seem like that big a deal. Here in central New York, I did not know anyone else with that story. The invitation to step into my calling felt unreal, like it should never have happened. Thoughts continued to echo in my mind: *If that other pastor had just stayed ... I bet some man out there said no to Jesus and so God had to ask me ... I'm God's second best for the job.* It felt as if stepping into my calling as a pastor might actually be God's Plan B, D, or Z but not Plan A for my life or church.

In my lowest moments during this time, I remember thinking, *If being a woman will prevent our church from reaching its fullest potential, I should just walk away. It isn't worth sacrificing the gospel.* My mind would go there because I had never seen a thriving, effective church with a female lead pastor.

---
I wish someone had told me, "Girl, you are not bigger than God's kingdom. Stop thinking so highly of yourself!"

---

It is easy to make ourselves bigger than Jesus in our life dreams and then use that as an excuse to self-sabotage or never even get started. The hidden lie we believe in this mess looks like, "I am not enough," but it is really also saying Jesus is not enough either.

Here is the bottom line: Jesus is either strong in our weakness or not. This isn't just true for some people! It is easy to see by our attitudes and mindsets whether or not we actually believe that reality. As a young pastor, I realized that what I thought about myself was a bigger limit than what other people thought about me. I was putting my own limitations and other people's opinions on the throne of my heart instead of walking in my identity in Christ by faith.

Impostor syndrome tried to steal my voice. The danger of believing that we are God's second best for a role is that we can start to discount ourselves, self-sabotage, or make up excuses or justifications for why we are not growing or stepping into the "more" God has for us. I found myself doing this, mostly subconsciously. Controlled failure can feel safer than discovering who we really are and what we are capable of rather than saying yes to God and taking a risk.

Thankfully, God began a healing journey in me by replacing the lies I believed with His truth. Jesus actually *is* enough for everything I face and am called to walk in. My identity in Christ and my calling are not accidental or a Plan B solution. Jesus showed me leaders and people from my past I needed to forgive, and He poured His healing into my identity. New mentors spoke God's courage and truth into my heart. My anxiety lessened and my physical health began to be restored as I chose to accept who God made me to be and caught fresh vision more than ever before. My vision shifted from trying to survive to learning to thrive. It was amazing to experience this transformation personally and see how it affected my church. We saw new growth and salvations! People in our community began to gain new confidence and faith in God. Vision is contagious. It is not magic—it is a lifelong adventure with Jesus, walking this out.

"'The thief comes only to steal and kill and destroy; I came so that they would have life, and have it abundantly'" (John

# God's Plan A

10:10). You are not God's second best for your life or calling. You are God's Plan A on earth—His abundant life poured out. Jesus's abundant life is not codependent on ideal life circumstances or a perfect life strategy. Instead, it is revealed through you and me as we surrender and share the specific giftings He has given us.

> There's no one who can take your place!
> You are uniquely designed to thrive in your
> calling and purpose on earth.

We do not have to look at our identity or calling in Jesus through the eyes of separation—trying to earn a connection or place at the table with Jesus. We can be secure in discovering who we are in Christ. We are not reinventing the wheel even if we feel like we are. There are women who have gone before us, from the time of the Old Testament to the time of Jesus until today.

A counselor I once interned with said that a common effect of being born out of wedlock can be a pattern of self-sabotage in life. If you have never been friends with or mentored by a woman who operated in the area of influence you feel called to, it can seem like you have been single parented into your dreams. Then we start self-sabotaging because it feels safer and more controlled than failing. But I am here to remind you that "to the fatherless he is a father. To the widow he is a champion friend. The lonely he makes part of a family. The prisoners he leads into prosperity until they sing for joy" (Psalm 68:5–6 TPT).

Your identity and strength to walk out your calling come from who you are in Christ and not how the world or your past defines you. There is just as much abundant life available today as there was 2,000 years ago when Jesus walked on our planet. Heaven is not running out! The question is, are we receiving it and letting it define what is possible? We are His body on earth.

God's truth sets us free from thinking we are a Plan B or Plan Z.

Be brave and ask yourself what today would look like if you actually believed you are God's Plan A for the world around you.

Girl, you are!

*Hannah Wakeman*

Senior Pastor, Thrive Church, Ithaca, New York
www.hannahwakeman.com

# Out in the Waters

## Stefanie Monk

Have you ever found yourself in the deep waters of uncertainty, hanging in the scales of life and death? When it is about you, that is one thing; but when it is about the children you have carried in your womb, you are in a whole different depth. My dear friend Stefanie talks about her journey where God met her in the deep waters.

---∞---

I grew up in the water: going to my grandparents' lake house; going to my aunt and uncle's beach house; floating the river; and my favorite, going to the waterpark!

When I was seven weeks pregnant with my first child, I went to the emergency room for bleeding. I left the ER devastated, thinking we were losing our child. For eight long days we grieved, then went for the follow-up with plans for what would happen next. To our surprise, not only did my bloodwork show that I was still pregnant, but the doctor also found her tiny, fluttering heartbeat.

I carried her for thirteen weeks, cautiously hopeful, and started dreaming of what her nursery would look like. We moved into a new apartment and were getting settled in and starting to unpack. I stopped to cook us dinner, and while I began cooking, I felt something happening. I ran to the bathroom. There was no bleeding, but I knew something was wrong. We went to Labor and Delivery this time since I was already twenty weeks along. It was determined what I felt was my water breaking. And though the doctor was hopeful that I could continue my pregnancy, there were many risks involved. Once again, we went home devastated.

One evening, while on bedrest, I read the story of Noah again. I thought of how devastating it must have felt to be the one chosen to build the ark. To have to endure the storm with so many unknowns. When the storms were over and the waters were receding, Noah began searching for a sign of life. He sent out a dove, and the third time he did, the dove brought back an olive branch. Noah knew that there was hope. So we decided to name our baby Olive.

Things were pretty uneventful for the first six weeks of bedrest, but at exactly twenty-six weeks, I began having complications. Within hours I was brought to the surgical room to have an emergency cesarean section as Olive's heartrate was going down and not coming back up quickly enough. At twenty-six weeks and one day, our 2-pound, 2-ounce baby was born.

We always knew she would spend a short time in the neonatal intensive care unit (NICU). Babies who live without amniotic fluid often have lung trouble. We had no idea about the ups and downs ahead of us. We watched babies come and go. We heard "two steps forward, one step back," over and over. We prayed Olive would avoid a heart procedure, and she ended up needing it. We prayed we could avoid a feeding tube, and she came home on a feeding tube. We spent 149 days in the NICU, but on June 3, we finally were able to bring her home.

One day, around the time she needed the heart procedure, I sat by her bed weeping. I looked at her tiny body and felt helpless, like there was nothing I could do for her. And the Lord brought me to a moment in my twenties when I was at my lowest point. My life was out of control, and I felt like I was beyond repair. After a particularly rough night, I drove my car and came within feet of going into a canal. I woke up so angry with God.

# Out in the Waters

As I sat by my tiny child's fiberglass bed, I cried because I knew He was there. He was not powerless, but it was one of those moments I had to live through. I saw that He hurts when I hurt. He loves me more than I could ever imagine. And He reminded me that He loved our tiny girl more than I could ever understand.

If there are two things I have carried with me through all of this, it is that He is sovereign and He loves me and has a purpose for my life. The same goes for everyone else. Through my journey of being a mother, there are so many times I have moments of a deep sense of feeling loved because I know how much I love my children, even when they are not their best selves, and God is a much better parent that I am.

Shortly after my earthly father suddenly passed, I was thrown into a whirlwind of figuring out what would happen next. My father was larger than life to me. He was funny, wise, and always had the advice I needed, and for a lot of days it felt hard to move on. I attended a conference for worship leaders, and as a friend spoke, she said a quote inspired by Charles Spurgeon's 1874 sermon "Sin and Grace" that will hold true for the rest of my life:

> "I have learned to kiss the waves that throw me up against the Rock of Ages."

So much of my life has felt like waves. Drawing me out and then drawing me back in. Mostly calm, but some days are so rough that I feel like I cannot pull myself up. But when you are tethered to the One who created the oceans, you learn to kiss the waves.

*Stefanie Monk*

# A Supernatural Experience

*Fear is not an option.*

## Traci Vanderbush

There are some big things going on in the world.

While pondering events, ramifications, and possibilities of how things could "go down," my mind was suddenly interrupted by a resounding, strong "Fear is not an option."

I began thinking back to my interactions with my grandmothers, great-grandmothers, and grandfathers. These people were some of the strongest I have ever known. There's a history of overcoming, enduring, and persevering that our generation has been privileged to not know, but my grandparents and their parents knew it too well, and deeply. Their tears were sown as strength to us today. We have our own battles, but many of our battles have come with conveniences and blessings others did not or do not have. Then comes the question:

> Could we do without the basics we have come to take for granted? Could we do without the securities we have known?

Bill and I have always lived a life that is very uncertain compared to many, but in that, we've learned that with God, it

# A Supernatural Experience

is always certain. Chapters and seasons of life teach us the power of letting go of security and being vulnerable in the loving hands of a heavenly Father who has good in mind for everyone. In the secret place, security and certainty are found even when difficulty abounds.

I spent some time researching my ancestors who knew war, bloody battles, food rations, mind-numbing hardships, and painful waiting. It is easy to think that we would never have to face what they faced. I mean, even the thought of living life without air conditioning is enough to challenge our existence. How far we have come, or how far backward have we gone on some levels? There is one safe place to dwell in this world: "He who dwells in the secret place of the Most High shall abide under the shadow of the Almighty" (Psalm 91:1 NKJV). But I wondered what those words really meant. I began to break down the words into bits I could begin to comprehend. To dwell ... to lodge in ... to make your residence in. Under the shadow ... the covering ... the refuge.

> The secret place is where I am made to abide.

In remembering this secret place, I recalled a supernatural event that happened in our home in 2007. We lived in Maui at the time, and I had been teaching my children about dwelling under the shadow of the Almighty. We read from Psalm 91 and focused on "He will cover you with his feathers, and under his wings you will find refuge" (Psalm 91:4 NIV) For three mornings in a row, we woke up to piles of white feathers outside our kids' bedroom doors. The first morning, we searched the house for birds. Nothing. No birds. The second morning, we started to understand. The third morning, we were ecstatic with laughter and thanked God for His covering. That afternoon, as we drove down the highway in Maui, Bill and I began to talk about the feathers that kept showing up. While we talked about it, a white feather flew into the car through the passenger's window, circled around in front of us, and then exited the driver's side. We laughed with delight. Our kids thought it was the coolest thing.

The next day, Bill was working his diving job, 90 feet deep in the ocean. I always prayed for him while he dove. He came home to show me what he had filmed that day (he did ocean videography). In the video, he was swimming with sharks. As he paddled past them into the deep blue, a big white feather floated right up to the camera, as if God was saying, "I am here too."

The covering is real and it is with each of you. When we know we are covered by the Almighty, there is no fear. Even in death and tragedy, the covering is real, but we only see it dimly or partly. Yet, assurance exists even in the darkest places. God's promise is never threatened by evil. He is not a man that he should lie (Numbers 23:19), and nothing has the power to destroy His Word.

I think we are living in a time when abiding in the secret place with God, abiding in the vine, listening to the voice of God, and remaining under God's shadow is necessary. And in that place, you will know that fear is not an option. You are a temple of the Holy Spirit (1 Corinthians 6:19–20). There is no fear in that temple.

Remain in the secret place of the Most High.

Abide under the shadow of the Almighty.

Fear is not an option.

Traci Vanderbush

# My Peach Story

## Shana Orser

You have likely lived long enough to realize that life isn't all peaches and cream, and perhaps this awareness might have even snuffed out your ability to taste the sweetness of living. We often allow the negatives to overtake the positives, and we forget to look at the world through eyes of childlike wonder.

One of my dearest friends Shana Orser always inspires me to remain in the childlikeness that Jesus spoke about in Matthew 18:3. The only way to see His kingdom is through the eyes of a child. And let me tell you, Shana is a mother, businesswoman, and minister who knows obstacles and challenges, but she's found that childlike faith is where you find the peaches and cream, the kisses from heaven that we often miss. I love this story about God's faithfulness in the middle of a bad day.

---

There is a song by the Brooklyn Tabernacle Choir that many times you will hear me singing for all to hear: "He's Been Faithful" written by Carol Cymbala. She sings about how God has always been faithful in every moment of pain, sorrow, fear, helplessness, or hopelessness; how every promise He has given is true no matter how impossible it seems; and how His love and mercy and faithfulness have remained constant despite doubt.

I think if you met me, you would say I smile a lot, that I am a positive person seeing things from a perspective that all things are possible in Christ. However, like so many women (mothers, sisters, daughters, friends) in certain moments, I struggle with a feeling of failure, sometimes even hopelessness. This story is about one of these moments.

The setting of this story was at a church camp in Chilton County, Alabama. My husband and I were there for five weeks with my children, ages two and eight, on a mission to watch Bridges of Faith ministry campground while the staff were in Ukraine. This particular week in July, at the last minute, I had to fill in as cook and dishwasher for a children's camp that was using the campground. And it happened to be the week of my birthday, July 9.

July 8 had been a busy day of cooking and cleaning, but it had also been especially discouraging as we had to use the little bit of money we had in our bank account to pay a credit card. And like a country song, we received word that our dog in Florida was missing. That evening I was super low. It seemed true that no matter how hard I tried, it was never enough. The lie of disappointing God and getting what I deserved was thriving.

Now, I love peaches—fresh juicy ones. Some of the counselors at the camp had been bragging to me that Chilton County peaches were the best in the world, "most definitely better than Georgia's." I had seen the little stands along the road and decided that was what I wanted for my birthday. But now there wasn't even enough cash to buy those perfect peaches. I said to God, "If you loved me, you would give me peaches for my birthday." Now, just in case you are ready to give me any credit for this being a fleece about my putting trust in God, let me be clear. My attitude was this: "If you loved me, you would give me peaches for my birthday, but you don't and you won't." My birthday morning was the last day of the camp, so it was a busy one of making breakfast and doing dishes. My sister called to wish me a happy birthday while I was in the middle of washing pots and pans. I proceeded to cry over the phone to her about our missing money and missing dog. About that time, I heard a knock on the counter around the corner. It was one of the camp counselors looking for me. He said, "We wanted to get you something to thank you for all you did for us, but we weren't sure what to get you, so we decided to bring you these." In his hands (you guessed it) was the most beautiful basket of peaches. Now I was crying because I realized God did hear and God did care. And I must affirm that God gives the best, juiciest peaches. They might be right about Chilton County too.

My husband was discouraged because he could not even buy his wife peaches for her birthday. As he was walking back to help me in the kitchen, he came upon our five-year-old daughter, Annika, eating a peach, the juice running down her arms. "Where did you get that peach?" he asked. "They are Mom's peaches," she said matter of factly. Danny came and we stood together, crying, as we stared at this gift from heaven. We knew it would all be okay.

By the way, money was given to us, and our dog was found and returned. That and thousands of other God moments is why I sing with that song that even though in my heart I have questioned and even failed to believe, yet He's been faithful, faithful to me.

If you are in one of those times when it seems everything is going wrong, or you are tired and weak, remember it is in our weakness that His strength is revealed. You cannot mess it up. He is just that kind, that big, and that good.

I am so grateful that it isn't up to me, my goodness, or my faith. It is about *His* goodness and *His* faithfulness.

You are loved!

*Shana Orser*

Destiny Ministries: www.destinymin.com
Antioch Aviation: www.bliss-air.com/Antioch_Aviation

# Being Present in His Presence

## God's Protection and Provision in Trials and Triumphs

### Carrie Cole

Have you ever worried about your future and the path to success? In a world that features success stories while shaping the picture-perfect, idealistic lifestyle, it is easy to plummet into turmoil and despair when we compare our situations to images of perfection. I have a dear friend Carrie Cole who excelled in her career, leading a very large company. What always stands out to me is the joy and childlike heart she carries. It is evident that the kingdom, not career, is where she has anchored herself. Now retired, Carrie has nuggets of gold to share about the trials and triumphs of life, and how to walk through them.

---

In the midst of trials and triumphs—that is basically life. We are either at the top of the roller coaster, down in the valley, or somewhere in between. And usually that is on a minute-by-minute basis! So how do we navigate this life journey? How do we stay calm in the storm and keep our focus in times of both trouble and joy?

# Being Present in His Presence

I retired a few years ago. It was one of those dream-come-true moments of retiring at a fairly young age after a successful career, from a worldly definition. I found myself in a strange and surprising time in which many people asked for my advice on how to have a successful career, and how I managed my life to get to the place where I now found myself. I gave out some quick career tidbits in response:

1. Do not judge "new" or "different" too soon. Have patience and be open-minded. Also, be grateful for new and interesting things to do as that's how you grow.
2. Work hard and always give it your best. Take ownership. You will never have regrets when you look back if you have done this.
3. If you believe you can add value, then engage and be part of the solution; do not wait for an invitation to be involved.

That's great surface-level advice from my Type A personality. It is even woven with some biblical truth. Do not judge, lest you be judged; love is patient, love is kind; work as though you are working for the Lord; help others.

But the truth is that none of that helped me navigate my journey. The real truth is I don't feel like some shiny example to behold. My life has been messy. I have made mistakes. I have had many forks in the road where big decisions had to be made. Sometimes the choice was right and sometimes it was way wrong. I have been on the mountaintop, and I have been so far in the valley that I thought my tears alone could drown me. Sounds pretty normal, very human, right? Along the way in this journey, however, I did truly discover what I believe is the only true help to navigate life: J-E-S-U-S!

I stay present with Jesus. Remembering what He has done for me and the freedom that comes from His grace is like a shot of adrenaline into the moment. I want to throw up my hands and smile. I feel childlike happiness. Suddenly, earthly things are dimmed appropriately and I can see the bigger, joyous view of eternal life, knowing God is so much more than anything else. He is more overwhelming, more appealing, more important. It is then that I feel unshakable. I can sit and hear God's gentle whisper. It is then that I can see the world from His view, where my desire is for His will to be done. Now, every decision seems so much easier to make. That's been the key to my life's journey.

My daughter asked me the other day, "Mom, how did you get there with your whole trust in God? I know we went to church as teens, but I don't remember praying or going to church as small children." Well, I grew up in a small town and went to church every week with my parents. I sang in the choir and knew all the Bible school stories, and that is where it ended. It was a small-town Sunday activity. I did not really accept Jesus as my Lord and Savior until I was thirty-seven. We were living in New Mexico without any family or close friends around us. My business venture had fallen apart, and I was experiencing the guilt, shame, and pain of a financial crisis that I had not only put myself and my husband into but also our three beautiful, small children. It was a scary and depressing time.

I was home one day to find the children playing, and the TV was on in the background. A TV evangelist happened to come on an advertisement and quoted John 3:16. "For God so loved the world, that He gave His only Son, so that everyone who believes in Him will not perish, but have eternal life." *Wham!* Just as this sentence was breathed out, my son—my beautiful, loved little boy—came running past me.

---
It was as if I had never heard those words before. "God loves me *so much* that He gave up *His Son* for me."

---

It was not an audible God moment, but it may as well have been one because He was there, He was present; I knew I

## Being Present in His Presence

believed, and I knew I was forgiven, and I knew my life would never be the same. It was a new day and nothing would be the same. I did not want the same. Somehow, I knew what life was all about—knowing God. And it was good.

So, I started trusting God to lead me, and I was fortunate to get a few job prospects in Denver. My husband and I packed up the kids and went there for a few days so I could interview and hopefully start on the path we believed God was leading us down. And it came to pass. I got a job offer with a very promising company and we were going to be okay. But God had other ideas.

While I was interviewing, my husband very clearly felt the Lord nudge him back in the direction of South Florida, where we had family and had previously lived. So, on the drive back home from Denver, when I thought we would be celebrating my new job and our new life in Denver, we were instead at another fork in the road. Denver or South Florida? Take the job or start a new search all over again? Is this really from God?

You can read many Bible stories to validate that His ways are higher and not always the easiest or most obvious choices, but we heeded the nudge and investigated South Florida. The rest of the details make for a very long story because it was all so incredible. The drive home from Denver to New Mexico was eight hours. By the time we were home, I had already spoken (phone interviewed) with the CFO of my previous employer in South Florida and scheduled a flight for that night so that I could seal the deal on an even better job in South Florida—where we would be surrounded by friends and family and where we all, ultimately, grew a deeper relationship with God. There were so many miracles along the way for this journey. It was completely obvious that God's hand was all over it. It should be no surprise that "Heed the nudge" has become a popular saying in our family.

> I believe that when you get vulnerable with
> God and quietly listen, He will guide you.

The other question I have been asked since I retired was "How did you know it was time? How did you know you had saved enough? How much is too much?" My response to these questions is this "How's your prayer life?" My belief, contrary to what many of my fellow financial planning professionals would sell to you, is that there is no perfect time or answer to these questions. Only God knows our future. You do not know the end result of this decision any more than the end result of any other decision when you make it. You do know, however, that God is with you and for you and will guide you. Look for signs around you—whether it's a family change, a work environment change, or a physical change. Most of all, go to Him with that same vulnerability and trust. It will become evident in His time. *Trust.* Then, step out in faith.

However, staying in God's presence, vulnerability in prayer, trusting, and stepping out in faith are especially hard amid a trial. It does not matter if the trial is a sickness, a financial crisis or a relationship issue; it is a time of chaos that is difficult to understand. It is even more difficult to remember that God is still present. I believe this is why God did and still does miracles and why He created us to have memories about how He gave us His word. The privilege in getting older is that I can look back at my life and see God's presence throughout, and His miraculous hand on, every moment of my life, turning all things for good.

I heard a wise person once say that a trial can be life-changing but it does not have to be life-ruining. It may not be what I ask for or what I expected. or the timing I would have liked, but God ultimately turned my bumps and bruises for good.

# Being Present in His Presence

Jesus died for our sins and rose so we could have the kind of relationship with the Father that was always intended (John 17:21). He even gave His Spirit to live inside us, and He intercedes for us in heaven 24-7. Allow Him to help you make decisions. God's waiting for you to talk with Him, and He wants you to listen to His gentle, loving whisper. Remember that He knows best. So, trade in your prayer for your will to be done to God's will be done. Do not be anxious but confident. If it is God's will, it will happen. Trust, step forward in faith, and keep God present—where He desires to be.

*Carrie Cole*

# Do It for Me

### Christine Zucker

I cannot say enough about the strength and fortitude of the woman you are about to hear from. She has been a friend and guide to me for many years. I have watched her walk through fire after fire, and in it all, I have seen her faith grow. Christine Zucker carries an endurance and perseverance that keeps me in awe. She is a teacher in one of the hardest, most challenging areas, and she is changing the lives of her students one by one. Lean in to hear a mighty truth she learned in the most bittersweet way.

---

When I first met my husband, I was somewhat dismayed at his messiness. I was organized and functioned best when things were clean and fresh. My apartment smelled like clean laundry and jasmine drifting into open windows on a summer's eve. His apartment smelled like the New York deli two floors down with just a hint of Penn Station thrown in for good measure. His creativity blossomed when he was surrounded by papers and cartons of Chinese takeout. I colored inside the lines and he preferred to make his own lines.

Now, unlike many women who go into marriage thinking they will change their intended into the person they most want him to be, I had no such illusions. I had met my future mother-in-law, and she was absolutely terrifying! If she couldn't get this man to clean up after himself, what chance did I have? So, I went into my marriage with eyes wide open, knowing I would

## Do It for Me

be doing the majority of the cleaning, organizing, and picking up.

Fast-forward two years and I was at my wits' end! Every day this man threw his underwear and clothing on the floor and walked away. Sometimes it was on the floor right next to the hamper! I got to the point where I would see his underwear and would be seething with rage. Of course, we talked about it but nothing changed. In a fit of temper, one day I cried out to Jesus and said, "Lord, can you pleeeaaase make this man pick up his underwear?" The Lord responded to me in my spirit and He simply said, "Will you pick up his underwear for Me?" I said, "Wait! I'm not the one leaving my underwear on the floor, Lord." He repeated, "Will you pick up his underwear for Me?" I hesitated momentarily and then said, "Yes." I immediately felt the roiling anger in my chest dissipate.

Every day I picked up his underwear and said out loud, "This is a sacrifice for you, Lord." Something miraculous started to take place. I started feeling joy when I saw his underwear and clothing on the floor. Picking it up was a mood lifter, an atmosphere changer. After a time, I started applying this to other things he did that annoyed me. Instead of being angry and feeling resentment, I decided to offer thanks. "Thank you, Lord, that my husband has such a great job that I can stay home with the kids. Thank you that he calls me five times a day. Thank you that he is a gentle, loving father to our kids."

---
That one thing changed everything.
---

Fast-forward eighteen years .... My husband was dying. He had cancer in every bone in his body. Movement was difficult for him, especially bending.

I went into our bedroom after I heard the shower turn off. I looked everywhere and there were no clothes on the floor. I suddenly felt panic. Where was he and where was his underwear? I ran through the house calling his name, and I found him in the laundry room. He was placing his dirty clothes in the washer. I said, probably louder than I should have, "What are you doing?" He turned slowly to face me with tears in his eyes and he said, "You have been picking my underwear off the floor for eighteen years and you have never said a word. I am so sorry, Chris." I burst into tears and wrapped my arms around him.

Through choked sobs, I told him I did not want him to pick them up, especially not now. I told him how Jesus used his underwear to drive contempt from my heart and replace it with love. We both stood there crying and laughing, holding on to each other.

Six weeks later, he left this world. I'd give just about anything to be able to pick up his dirty clothes one more time.

Familiarity does not have to breed contempt. It can breed love, too, if we let it.

*Christine Zucker*

# Snakes in the Fire

## Bethany Martin

Are you afraid to face snakes? In this world, we have to face snakes, whether literally or figuratively. Personally, I hate snakes so much that I have spent time in prayer asking God to eliminate venomous ones from this planet. Ridiculous prayer, I know, but I am passionate about my dislike for them. My desert-dwelling son, on the other hand, tries to convince me that they serve a good purpose, but I have a hard time accepting that.

My friend Bethany Martin, a powerful prophetic worshipper and founder of the Heart of Texas House of Prayer, shares her own dislike of snakes, and she ties it into a profound truth. Her story is going to empower you greatly, so get ready to receive.

———∞———

I was raised on a bayou in Houston, and we frequently had poisonous water moccasins come into our backyard. Our little dachshund dog would make a certain "snake bark," and we would run to see what snake had come by. One summer, my parents counted thirty-three water moccasins in our yard! My mother was petrified of snakes, so when I was about eleven or twelve years old, Mom would send me out to grab a hoe and kill the snakes. This began my strong dislike (okay, hatred) of snakes.

Recently, I was reading in Acts 27 and 28 how the apostle Paul was on his way to Rome to fulfill a prophetic word given to him. I feel there are some lessons in this for us. Paul had just spent a couple of years in prison based on false accusation.

Being falsely accused is rough enough, but Paul told the group taking him to Rome that they should have followed his advice and not set sail from Crete (Acts 27:22–25). Then he told them to stop fasting, eat something, and keep up their courage, because they were all going to crash on an island ... but good news, no one would die! Sometimes the truth is not well received. It is interesting that Paul was not delivered from the shipwreck with signs and wonders, but God did bring him through to fulfill the word over his life to go to Rome.

Back to the snake. As I reread Acts 27 and 28, there were several key things God highlighted to me.

1. Paul was on assignment to Rome based on a word from God. It was going to happen because God said it, but it was delayed. Paul must have been discouraged or concerned that it might not come to pass. Sure enough, Paul ended up on a ship heading to Rome from the place of captivity because of a false accusation. **Do not be discouraged in the delay.**

2. After several shipwrecks to get there, they jumped ship and landed on the island of Malta. Acts 28:3 says, "But when Paul had gathered a bundle of sticks and laid them on the fire, a viper came out because of the heat and fastened itself on his hand." It is interesting that *Paul* did not start the fire, but he added fuel to the fire that was there. The fire caused the snake to manifest. **Do not be surprised when we stir up the fire of God in our regions that it may also stir up the enemy.**

3. The Greek word for viper in that passage is *echidna*. It is interesting to me that it is the *same* word Jesus used for the religious leaders of His day in the Gospels. In Matthew 12:34 Jesus says, "You offspring of vipers, how can you, being evil, express any good things? For the mouth speaks from that which fills the heart." **I believe**

## Snakes in the Fire

**the snake here represents the evil religious system, the very one that falsely accused and imprisoned Paul.**

4. Another important lesson for us is that the snake's mouth, which represents the enemy's words, did *not* harm or stop Paul. These religious snakes that want to bite us with their words, and people who falsely accuse us, cannot stop us unless we agree with them. *God will have the last word over us!* The snakebite did not stop Paul from doing what God called him to do. *He did not focus on the snake.* **Fear of the religious spirit has kept us from confronting it because we don't want it to strike us back.** I have felt that way myself at times and have personally been bitten by the snake of religion.

5. I also felt this was an exhortation to us as God's people to not be focused on the biting, false words of the religious or governmental snakes, nor allow the words of the naysayers to hurt us or slow us down. Instead, **we must continue forward to fulfill the words God has written for us in our books (Psalm 139:16).**

6. Lastly, the strategy to overcome the snake was to shake it off and fling it into the fire. I love this! The snake bit Paul on the hand, he flung it off into the fire, and everyone around him expected him to puff up and fall over dead. To their surprise, he was unaffected, so they assumed he was a god. Imagine you have spent two years of your life imprisoned, based on false words against you; you have just been through a nightmare of being shipwrecked; and you finally get to the place of promise and a snake bites your hand. Paul just flung that snake into the fire and kept going. **The same fire that caused the snake to manifest was the weapon that took it out!**

The Greek word for shook is *apotinasso* and it means "to shake off, to brush off." It is the same phrase used when Jesus sent the twelve disciples out to proclaim the kingdom of God. "'As for all who do not receive you, when you leave that city, shake the dust off your feet as a testimony against them'" (Luke 9:5).

Right after the snakebite, Paul went to a governmental leader's house and healed his dad. Acts 28:8 says, "The father of Publius was lying in bed afflicted with a recurring fever and dysentery. Paul went in to see him, and after he prayed, he laid his hands on him and healed him." It is interesting that **the same hand that got bitten by this snake was used by God to bring healing!**

What have you stopped doing because of words of accusation or hurtful words against you? We need to shake off the religious spirit and the ones who have not received us so we can continue to move forward and impact our regions with signs and wonders of the kingdom of God. The very thing that caused the snakes (the religious spirits) to come out in the first place was the more intense fire, but it will also be what takes out the snakes in our lives.

> Prayer: *Lord Jesus, let us not be held back by fear. Let us shake off the dust of those who have not received us and walk forward unhindered. Cause any hurtful words or accusations against us to fall into the fire of Your voice and be burned up so we can fulfill all You have planned for us.*

*Bethany Martin*

Founder of The Heart of Texas House of Prayer
www.hothop.org

# The Power of a Story

## Christine Zucker

I am going to tell you a tale that I have retold a million times because it has helped me through a very difficult time that many women experience. It is not an easy story to tell, and it certainly was not easy to live through, but this story imparted many gifts to me that I was going to need down the road to keep going.

When I was thirty years old, I was married to the man of my dreams. I had a beautiful baby girl who was a year old, and I was pregnant with my second child. Life was everything I ever wanted it to be. We were happy.

One night I had a dream. In this dream, I was standing in my kitchen washing dishes and my baby girl was playing on the floor with her toys when the doorbell rang. I dried my hands on a dishtowel and went to the front door. We lived in Seattle, so it was cold and rainy outside. As the door swung open, I looked down and there on my doorstep was a baby in a wicker basket. I looked up and down the street, but it was deserted, so I picked up the basket and brought it inside. I immediately called the police. I said, in somewhat of a panic, "Someone left a baby on my doorstep and I don't want you to think I took someone's baby. I have a baby of my own!" I was babbling and nervous. This was unknown territory to me.

The police officer said, "Could you keep the baby for three days? We will have someone watching the house. Typically, the real mother will come back by the third day." I said I would since I already had the baby gear required to take care of the baby. I hung up the phone and said out loud, "Lord, what should we call this baby?" In the dream there was a very loud and audible response. He said, "The baby's name is Jesse." In the dream, the hair on my arms stood up. Just then I saw an envelope nestling next to the baby, and I picked it up and opened it. The plain white card simply said, "The baby's name is Jesse." So I thought, *Okay. Confirmation.* Then I reached down to pick up the baby—a beautiful, chubby, golden-haired cherub that had that intoxicating baby scent wafting up from his downy head. I melted into the embrace of this little head on my shoulder. At that moment, the Lord said audibly, "Christine, you can't keep this baby." I said, "Oh, okay, Lord," and I placed the baby back in the basket. Just then I looked up and a white tornado was in my kitchen, and as it hit me, everything went white and then black.

I sat straight up in bed trying to smother the scream that was on my lips. I shook my husband and said, "Wake up! I just had a really weird dream and I need to tell you about it." He groaned and asked if there was coffee. *Ugh!* I told him there would be coffee later. I started telling him about the dream and he was largely nonplused, but I couldn't shake it. It was like it was present even in my waking hours. I wrote it down because it was bothering me so much.

Three days later, I woke up excited because it was the morning of my thirty-first birthday. We had big plans for the day. I ran to the bathroom and was stopped dead in my tracks. I was bleeding. I was eleven weeks along. I called my OB and she said, "Put your feet up and if the bleeding increases or you have pain, come to the ER." It did increase, and we went to the

# The Power of a Story

hospital. The ultrasound guy told us the baby was gone. He thought I must have passed it at home. We cried.

On our way home, my husband said, "Hey, remember that dream you had? Wasn't the baby's name Jesse?" I said, "Yes." After a pause, he said, "I think we are supposed to name the baby Jesse." When we got home, I looked the name up and it means "The Lord exists."

We spent the weekend grieving and on Sunday night, my husband reminded me that he was supposed to go on a business trip to California in the morning. He offered to cancel, but I said, "Why? Are you going to stay home and mope with me? Go on your trip. I'll be fine." But on Monday afternoon, I started to have contractions. I called my OB office and they said that it was normal after a miscarriage. I had an appointment with my doctor the next morning, so I resigned myself to the pain and decided to live with it until the following day.

The next day, I went to my appointment and the doctor said my cervix was closed and everything looked good. As soon as she got the bloodwork back, she would know if a DNC was necessary. I went home and fed my little girl her lunch, which she promptly smashed all over her face and hair. As I was carrying her upstairs for a quick bath, I felt my body explode. I looked down and there was blood all over the staircase. I kept going and every few feet, my body was expelling large amounts of blood. I managed to get to the bathroom with my baby girl in tow but quickly realized I needed help. I called the OB and they very condescendingly said, "Ma'am, you were just here. It is normal to have heavy bleeding after a miscarriage." The nurse hung up! I called my best friend at work and she came right over. I put on a pad and sweatpants and sat on two towels in her car. By the time we got to the doctor's office, I had bled through it all. I walked in and said, "I need to see the doctor. It's an emergency." She told me to take a seat and that I would have to wait. I told her if I sat down, she would have to throw her chair out because there was already a puddle of blood at my feet. She looked down and yelled, "Why didn't you tell me!" I said, "I have been trying to tell you!"

They rushed me to the procedure room and the doctor came flying in with her hair on fire, asking what happened. I said, "I don't know!" She took one look and said to me, "I am so sorry, sweetie, but I have to give you a DNC with no meds or you are going to bleed out. I promise I'll give you something when it's over, but I have to stop the bleeding now." I nodded. At the first wave of searing pain, everything went white, then suddenly black.

When I came to, the doctor was holding my baby in her hands. She said, "They missed this at the hospital. This is called a catastrophic miscarriage. Your baby was stuck in the cervix." She later told me that sometimes after a catastrophic miscarriage, women cannot conceive again. I was traumatized. I was grief-stricken, and I was heartbroken. I left her, feeling the weight of her pronouncement over my life. This was not the life I had dreamed of. Then the words "dreamed of" echoed in my mind. I felt them reverberate off the inner recesses of my spirit. I had dreamed this. This was *exactly* what I dreamed.

I pulled out my journal and read what I had written. Every part of that dream came true, right down to my passing out. It was definitely a warning dream, but there was something much deeper there.

---
God let me hold my baby before He took him back.

---

He let me know what was about to happen, not just to say, "Hey, some bad stuff is about to go down and your life isn't going to be a fairy tale. See ya!" God tells us things to give us hope and trust in Him.

# The Power of a Story

So, part of my journey through the grief process was learning to offer thanks and believing God always has the best in store for us, even when it does not match what doctors say or what we thought our life would be like.

Habakkuk said it best when he said, "Even if the fig tree does not blossom, and there is no fruit on the vines, if the yield of the olive fails, and the fields produce no food, Even if the flock disappears from the fold, and there are no cattle in the stalls, yet *I will triumph in the LORD, I will rejoice in the God of my salvation*" (Habakkuk 3:17–18, emphasis mine).

Did I have any other children? I did. My daughter Ariel was born on the same date that I had the dream, three days before my birthday. I found out I was pregnant with my son on the day Jesse was due to be born. On that day, the Lord said to me, "See, I have given you back double for what you lost." He always does. He always will.

If you are in a dark place, He will come through for you. He will walk through it with you. He will give you beauty for all your ashes.

*Christine Zucker*

# Healed and Delivered

### Stephanie Tate

Have you ever battled for enough faith to believe something you can't see with your eyes? Or the faith to believe for the opposite of what your eyes are seeing? When the mountains seem to keep coming and the negative diagnosis is looming, there's a beautiful place for your heart to dwell, and that is in knowing that God is good, no matter what. My friend Stephanie Tate is a mother and nurse. She shares this personal story of walking through a storm only to discover that God is still good.

---∞---

It was a hot summer day in July. My husband and I were fishing with our son Tyler, who was in his early twenties at the time. As he was casting his line, I noticed an unusual lump under his arm. Being a registered nurse, I thought perhaps it was an enlarged lymph node or abscess. As I began full mom-triage nurse mode with a hundred questions and an examination of his arm, he mentioned it had been getting bigger for the last month but had dismissed it; perhaps he banged it on something. I did not like the sound or presentation of any of this and encouraged him to see his doctor first thing Monday morning.

## Healed and Delivered

He started with one doctor who passed it off as an abscess. This did not sit right, so he saw another family physician, who agreed and ordered a sonogram. After waiting for days on a result, it came back as inconclusive. Less than ideal, and unfortunate. My heart began to sink as I knew what this could mean. This was the start of many nerve-racking months.

With hope in my heart, peppered with optimistic thoughts, which was half rooted as a facade of strength for Tyler and half rooted in denial that this could be anything significant—as he was a young, healthy man with his whole life ahead of him—with no understanding what this lump was, the physicians proceeded to MRIs, which led to a diagnosis of a neuro sheath tumor. The diagnosis was a double-edged sword. We finally knew what it was, but it was less than ideal for a diagnosis.

The world seemed to stop for a moment, and then my ER nurse's trauma response or mom mode quickly kicked in; however, I had no clue what this tumor was. As we learned very quickly, these types of tumors are very uncommon, particularly in the arm. Because of this, we began the journey of seeing multiple different doctors and surgeons. Doctor visits and tests became a full-time job, and then the mental, emotional, and physical stress of the unknown went to work in the after-hours.

Continued barriers occurred, from trying to facilitate surgeons that could handle his case and time limits to financial expenses. He endured multiple biopsies that had to be repeated due to inconclusive results, and other ongoing tests. It was an exhausting roller coaster.

After months of tests and not knowing if this was benign or cancerous, and trying to make sense of possible outcomes for a young man who had his whole life in front of him, there were many sleepless nights. As a mother I felt helpless, but I had to be strong, and I felt like I had to keep it together for everyone.

> I was thankful for my faith; God had been with me since a young age and had been faithful and real in my life. But how was this going to play out for my son?

His walk with God had not been the same as mine. Would God meet him or help him the same way? I had to believe that despite where Tyler was with God, God loved me enough and knew the love of a mother; surely that would be enough. So I would pray, standing on God's promises that He spoke to me about my son. I would remind myself of all the times God had moved in his life, and I tried to dig up any encouragement and hope.

A dear woman gave me the scripture Psalm 107:19. I posted it on the fridge and declared it daily: "Then they cried out to the LORD in their trouble; He saved them from their distresses." Despite all this, fear and helplessness carried on with its hostile takeover of my family. I was in a full-fledged war of the mind and spirit.

One night the Holy Spirit reminded me of a word He had spoken to me years earlier, when I had felt guilty about being a working mom. He said, "Where you stop, I pick up." I initially thought He meant that He filled the gaps, picked up the pieces, passed the baton in the parenting race. However, He showed me a deeper meaning that night, saying that if I would stop wrestling with fear and anxiety and declare that all of this was in His hands, and truly give it to Jesus, then He would pick up the issue and handle it, but that I had to stop and walk away from the wrestling match. After all, I couldn't do any more. This was all out of my control!

So, I felt like Abraham must have when bringing his son to the altar. I said over and over, "Whatever the outcome, I know You love him (Tyler) more, and I will praise You, no matter what." I continued to pray for the best outcome, and when fear came to wrestle, I reminded myself, *God has him, no matter the outcome; stop and walk away from the wrestling match.* I realized no matter the relationship status that Tyler had with God, it did not matter because I knew God loved Tyler more than I could. I also knew God was and is good, despite my lack of understanding of why bad situations occur in life. It was not up to me to make sense of all this.

> It was not my job to plead to God for favorable outcomes. It *was*, however, my job to stop and let God work through this, and no matter the outcome, praise Him.

Fall came, and we were miraculously able to get an appointment with a top surgeon, one of the top three in the country who specialized in treating this rare tumor. Additionally, he was located in our state and was even in our network for insurance! These types of surgeons' schedules are booked for months out, and we were able see him in just a few months. All of this was a miracle in and of itself. (If you work in healthcare, or spend enough time maneuvering through it, you know what I mean!)

In November, Tyler was set for surgery. The complexity of this surgery meant that he could potentially lose the function of his arm. He likely would never play music and sports again and would live with some disability. With the removal of the neuro sheath tumor, we would also be able to confirm its pathology, concluding whether it was cancerous or benign. The worst outcome in front of us would be the loss of his arm *and* a cancer diagnosis, which typically leads to a long journey of challenges with poor outcomes.

In our hotel the night before surgery, we did not sleep much—we were waiting for the alarm to go off as we had to arrive early at the hospital. From registration to pre-op, the anxiety was high, but trusting God was really where the rubber was meeting the road in faith. By 9:00 a.m., I had prayed with Tyler and reminded him that he was in God's hands, and that I loved him. Then Tyler was off to surgery. I found a quiet place and cried out to God, praying for healing my son. With no tears left, I pulled myself together and sat in the waiting room, fighting to keep my mind in God's peace.

Eight hours later, and early in the evening, the surgeon came to the waiting room. He told me that Tyler had lost a lot of blood and the tumor was wrapped around many vital vessels, nerves, and muscles, and that it was worse than anticipated. However, he (the surgeon) felt confident he had gotten everything. He also said he would send the tumor to pathology. He noted that Tyler would likely not feel anything (if he was to gain feeling again) for months, possibly up to a year. The prognosis was not looking good, but we were thankful he had made it through surgery and was awake.

Over the next two weeks, Tyler had a wound complication that thankfully healed. However, things started to look brighter. His biopsy came back benign, praise the Lord! Then, around Christmas, Tyler started to gain full feeling and function of his hand and arm, and he began playing the guitar. Tears came, praise God, as this was the best outcome—God's outcome! I was quickly reminded of Psalm 107:19–21:

> Then we cried out, "Lord, help us! Rescue us!" And he did! God spoke the words "Be healed," and we were healed, delivered from death's door! So lift your hands and give thanks to God for his marvelous kindness and for his miracles of mercy for those he loves! (TPT).
>
> YAHWEH, you are my soul's celebration. How could I ever forget the miracles of kindness you've done for me? (Psalm 103:2 TPT)

# Healed and Delivered

I don't know why situations happen to people, and I have concluded that it is not my job to try to make sense of it or understand it. However, in life's situations and their outcomes, stop and rest in God's love, as He is good and gracious no matter what we believe.

We cannot earn His love or buy it. No matter the condition or what we see or feel, stop and remember who He is and what His love can do.

*Stephanie Tate*

# Spiritual Grit

### Ronda Olson

Ladies, you're no strangers to the truth that walking through this life requires "spiritual grit." I love the way that my friend Ronda Olson titled her story because it is so appropriate. We all need it! Most of us come to that place where we want to check out of a situation or just plain give up. You must hear the testimony of this incredible woman.

---∞---

Let me start by introducing you to a bit of my story. I grew up learning about Jesus, but I could not connect. I must have prayed that sinner's prayer hundreds of times throughout my childhood yet left feeling no different. This changed one day—when I was fourteen—on a communion Sunday that was no different from any other monthly communion Sunday. The pastor did not say anything different from usual. Suddenly, I felt the warmth of God's love pour over me from head to toe like a warm oil flowing from heaven. The overwhelming power of His love could not be resisted. I was compelled to say yes to Him with my whole being.

The manifestation of emotion was not normal in our little denominational church, yet here I was letting everything flow from my eyes and nose and barely keeping my mouth from sobbing uncontrollably. I felt no condemnation but was simply drawn by His love.

Once our row was dismissed to go to the altar to receive the cup and wafer from the deacons, I ran to the altar. I may have been a bit of a spectacle. From the looks my mother was giving me, I knew I was, but I did not care.

It was not long before my God-fearing father instilled some downright legalism into my experience. About two weeks after this experience with the love of Jesus and meeting the Holy Spirit head on, my father asked me, "Have you told your friends at school about Jesus?" Being the introvert I was, and am, I replied with an emphatic *no*! He proceeded to quote to me: "But whoever denies me before men, I also will deny before my Father who is in heaven" (Matthew 10:33 ESV). This instilled in me a heavy dose of condemnation.

At this point, in my mind and heart I said to myself, as if I had thrown my hands up in my mind, *That is it. I'm out*! For the next two years, I searched for other Christians who walked in the truth of the *love* I had met, who walked and talked with Holy Spirit. To my dismay, I couldn't find any within my circle. I went searching further but found none there either. By sixteen, I had completely walked away from the Lord.

I will fast-forward over many years and experiences. By the time I hit thirty, I was married with one child and living a full-on biker lifestyle. Drinking and drugging, clinically depressed, and unsatisfied, I sensed that I was at a crossroads of life or death. I want to be clear, I was not suicidal, but I could sense I needed to choose. I worshipped my marriage—not my husband but the marriage itself. I was determined to make our marriage work no matter what. I was fully committed.

As the years passed by, I could sense the presence of Holy Spirit gently nudging me to return to my first love, the *love* I was introduced to on that Sunday morning so many years ago. I continued to say no because I could not see how it would work. What would happen in our house? How could we coexist in the same household living completely opposite lifestyles? What would become of my marriage? My marriage!

> Over all the years, He had never left me.

I walked the other way, but Holy Spirit never left me and continued to woo me over all those years. Holy Spirit spoke to me in times of danger and warned me. I did not always listen, yet I was protected. I was never forced, yet the invitation became stronger and more pressing.

When I finally said "I trust you, Jesus," I meant it with everything in me. If it cost me everything, I would give it up with open hands. This is where I became aware of possessing spiritual grit. I did not know I had it, but it was there.

Whenever we overcome something, we have authority in that very area. In my formative years, I did not have the grit to press forward in my relationship with Holy Spirit within the constraints of legalism and peer pressure, but with the experience of years of choosing life over death, I had developed this determination that I refer to as spiritual grit. It grew out of my desperation for life and health while living in a very unhealthy situation.

My marriage, in all reality, had become a great business arrangement rather than a healthy and intimate relationship. We did not fight or hate one another, we just worked together in our household like a business partnership.

Let's explore the definition of grit: a piece of sand or stone, courage and resolve, strength of character. You ever get a rock in your shoe? This rock has the effects of grit on your foot. When you empty your shoe, what may have felt like a big rock was actually a small pebble. When we walk out who we truly are with resolve, this may cause others to feel as though we are the rock in their shoe. This certainly became the case in our home. But also, think of a tiny piece of sand that gets inside the clam shell; this irritating piece of grit is precisely what becomes a beautiful pearl over time.

# Spiritual Grit

As I grew in my relationship with Jesus, the depression was displaced with His presence. Intimacy with Holy Spirit gave me peace which truly does surpass my understanding (Phillipians 4:4–7)

As I grew in my relationship with the Trinity, I became more confident in who I was created to be. As I have traveled the road of life with the Father, Son, and Holy Spirit, I have had seasons when this steadfastness has served me well. I now know that even in times when I feel forsaken, the Lord keeps me. In the ebb and flow of life in Him, there are times of hiddenness and manifestation. There are mountaintop experiences as well as valleys. This is sometimes by design.

As I look back over a considerable amount of life, it has been in the hard or hidden times that the Lord has done His deeper work in me. When I do not hear or feel Him in the fashion that I desire, I know that He is very busy on my behalf. He does not abandon or forsake me, and He is always working things for my good. In extended seasons of hiddenness, I can remember what He has done when I was unaware, and I imagine what He is doing currently.

Spiritual grit is simply agreeing with His faith for any situation, big or small, knowing that I am His beloved, the apple of His eye, His poem, and His daughter, and He is a good Father who keeps me.

> Don't forget to look for angels and the Father's gifts. They are all around you.

*Ronda Olson*

www.impactministries-kingmakers.org

# Carrying Promise

## Sarah Morales

Oh, my goodness, dear friend. Have you ever carried a promise that seemed to be lost forever? Have you been alone in the darkness, the lonely nights? Ever thought that no one could possibly understand? Meet Sarah Morales, my friend, a mother, and a profoundly powerful worship leader. She has a story to share with you.

---

My lifelong dreams were to sing, serve the Lord in worship, get married, and be a mom. Specifically to carry babies. I wanted the whole experience. There is something about the moment when you finally find out you are having a baby—everything changes.

Before I ever felt different, the awareness that I carried life shifted how I carried myself. My first pregnancy ended in a miscarriage. And although the miscarriage occurred pretty early into the pregnancy, it was heartbreaking because of my awareness of the life I had been carrying. I have had three full-term babies since, but because of a complication in delivery with my first baby, all of my babies have been born via C-section. That was not my plan. Although I am in full support for moms who choose C-sections, it just wasn't my first choice.

> I remember feeling like a complete failure because I could not deliver my firstborn naturally.

I was later informed by the doctors and nurses that the C-section saved my baby's life as the cord was short and wrapped around his neck, and it would have choked him in delivery. I realized I had a choice. I could mourn the process or delight in the answer to my greatest heart's desire. I made the decision with the next babies to accept and find joy in the "out of the box" method of delivery.

Just like the birthing process, each promise of God is carried differently. Each one requires something different. Our job is to care for ourselves and to listen closely for the needs of the "baby" we are carrying.

If you have had a baby or are close to someone who has, you come to understand there are so many lonely, unseen parts of pregnancy—especially in the early weeks, when you may know but no one else is aware of what you are carrying. Yet you continue to steward that little one inside you with the joy, hope, and promise of what lies within and before you.

So much about pregnancy and birthing reminds me of what it feels like to carry promises and words yet fulfilled. This resonates deeply with me in my season of waiting to see my dreams and desires come to fruition. The Bible is full of people who were given words and promises from God and had very long seasons of waiting and wondering. Some of our patterns in the waiting find us questioning and doubting if we heard correctly. The thought comes in that maybe *the promise* was for someone else. I feel passionate in this season to encourage the body and to speak to hearts that may be losing hope.

I have spent the last few weeks thinking of Mary the mother of Jesus. Jesus, the Messiah, had been prophesied about hundreds of years before He actually was born. When He came, it was to the most unlikely person in the most unlikely way. I have begun to ponder some of these things in my heart. The Lord was looking for a yes that would be given in complete surrender, with total trust and without fear. He needed someone who would keep the promise safe no matter the cost.

We know the story, but there were some things highlighted to me in regard to carrying and birthing promise. Mary's yes did not make her popular; it made her open to criticism. Joseph, who also decided to say yes, accepted the challenge to be a father to Jesus, the Son of God, without really knowing what would happen. But in the word and promise he was given, he was also given everything he needed to support Mary.

> God is looking for those with a *yes* in their hearts, those who will not abort the promise. He is looking for those who will not give up and who will be open to how He decides to bring the promise about.

When it was time to deliver the promise of Jesus, Mary and Joseph were sent away from the comforts of home and family, and placed on a unique journey. Jesus would be born in a place where there was "no room." They were not sent to wide-open doors and grand hospitality.

The story of Jesus's birth we hear about is mostly set in the night hours, in the darkness of a cold, lowly cave. The angels' heralded lowly shepherds in a cold, dark field. A star in the night led the wise men on a journey across lonely deserts to find the King. I began to think about that night and the lowly place where Jesus was birthed and where the announcement was made. It wasn't done in broad daylight and in the temple or a palace. It wasn't the Radio City Music Hall version of the nativity, full of pomp, circumstance, and pageantry. It was completely different from what people had waited for or expected. Yet it was the most powerful, precious answer and fulfillment to His promise we could ever receive.

I felt the Lord stir my heart in the midst of this beloved story. Be faithful to steward your dream and promise when it is not popular and when no one is looking. Be open to how God will bring things about in your life while He is perfecting your promise and making you ready. Meet Jesus in the night seasons and keep your gaze focused as you search Him out. The light in the darkness allows us to shut all other things out and to see what we need to see. Let the light of heaven and promise of Jesus invade your heart as you read. Be encouraged as you co-labor to see His kingdom established through your life!

*Sarah Morales*

Worship Leader/Songwriter
www.throneandhome.com

# It's Never Too Late!

## Ronda Vanderbush

Now here is a lady who will inspire you to pursue the call of God on your life no matter how old you are. Ronda Vanderbush is my mother-in-law. She's known me since I was five years old! I have seen her live a life of commitment to God's Word, willing to wait on Him and hear what He has to say.

One thing I am passionate about is the ability for the older and younger generations to work together, respect and honor each other, and gain wisdom in the sharing. The generation gap must be closed! I truly believe that we forfeit blessings when we disregard other age groups. That's why I especially value this story from my mother-in-law, who sees age as no barrier. You will be inspired as you read.

———∞———

From the time I was a young child, I had a deep interest in missions. My father was a pastor, and he would often have missionaries come speak at our church. Afterward, they would come to our home for dinner, and I would listen to their stories. I admired these missionaries and loved getting to know them. Our denomination supported a number of couples in South America, and we learned all about their lives in the

# It's Never Too Late!

field and the culture of the people they worked with. I loved all of it.

My grandfather came to live with us for a time when I was in first grade, and he loved missions too. His room was upstairs in our house, and I would climb up there to see him, knowing that he would get out his big book all about Africa and a missionary named David Livingston. We would look through the book with pictures of the African people and the many types of wild animals that lived in Africa. I was so intrigued by it all that it never left my heart.

As the years sped by and it was time for college, I just naturally planned on being a schoolteacher, but my dream was to teach in Africa. I taught in Vancouver, Washington, for nine years, and then I met a handsome single evangelist who came to Vancouver to preach at a camp meeting where I just happened to be playing the piano. So you can probably guess the rest of the story! A year later, we married and took off on a thirty-four-year journey of evangelism in North America, as well as going to various mission fields, which I loved. But we never did get to Africa.

After Henry passed away in 2013, I moved to Texas to be near my son and his wife and my two grandchildren, and while living there, Bill took me to a meeting where a missionary from Africa named Heidi Baker was speaking. I was deeply touched by her heart of love and her commitment to her calling, and at the close of the meeting, Bill took me up to meet her. Like she did to everyone, she gave me a big hug. I told her I would love to visit the field in Africa and wondered if there could be anything I could do to help. I will never forget what she said, without hesitation.

---

She said, "You could love the children."
And I thought, *I sure could*!

---

*Women in Christ*

A few years later, I noticed that another evangelist named Randy Clark had a ministry of sending teams to different mission fields to become acquainted with the culture and perhaps feel a call to become a missionary as their life's work. I noticed there was a team going to Mozambique—where Heidi and Rolland Baker lived—so right then and there, I decided to sign up for that two-week trip to Pemba, Mozambique.

The majority of those who go on these trips are younger people. A few are middle-aged, but I was seventy-nine! However, I was not going to let that stop me. The worst that could happen was they would turn me down. But a few weeks later I received the letter that I was accepted, and talk about excited! That was in 2018. I was so excited that the twenty-hour trip to Johannesburg did not bother me a bit. The next day we boarded the smaller plane for Pemba, and as I looked out the window at the jungle below, I felt like crying; it was like a lifelong dream coming true. And then as the plane made a turn, the beautiful sea-blue Indian Ocean came into view. It was breathtaking!

The next two weeks were full of wonder and love. I received an impartation that I have never gotten over: how anything could be so fulfilling and glorious when most of the time there was no electricity, no water, and only rice and beans twice a day. But there were tons of children to love! The greatest blessing was what this experience did in my heart and life. And one thing I knew—I wanted to return as soon as possible.

It was on the way to the airport, on the day we were to fly back to the States, when we heard the news—beheadings were happening just a couple of hours from the mission base. And because of this, the province eventually had to be closed to visitors. Our group was the last to get in and get out before they shut down. In the five years since I was there, many people have been beheaded, hundreds of churches have been burned, and hundreds of villages totally destroyed, and yet the converts to

# It's Never Too Late!

Christianity have so far exceeded the million converts that came to Christ in the preceding twenty-five years that the missionaries are praising the Lord and giving glory to Him in spite of the hell they have gone through.

You say, "Wasn't that scary? Surely you wouldn't think of going again!" My trust is in God. If God says "Go," I want to go! If the province of Cabo Delgado opens up again, which many believe will happen, I would love to go there. But there are plenty of other mission bases that are safe and open for visitors. All this to say, if you have had a desire deep in your heart, maybe for years, to do something for God, and now you think there is no way because the years have crept up on you and you feel like you have missed it for good,

---
I want you to know *it's never too late!*

---

I went to Mozambique to be a blessing, but I came home with much more than I gave out—something I totally did not expect. And it has marked me ever since. I would not trade that experience for anything! So, take the plunge, trust God, jump out of the boat, and you will find yourself doing what you never thought you could do. God will bless you and enrich you, and He will never, ever let you down.

It's never too late!

*Ronda Vanderbush*

Minister and Cofounder of Faith Mountain Ministries
https://billvanderbush.com/fm-ministries

# Embrace the Journey

### Bettina Grzeskowiak

Throughout my life, I have met thousands of warrior women, conquerors, and carriers of the impossible. I wish I could write a chapter on each of them, but if I did, this book would become volumes and volumes of massive encyclopedia-thick books that would break any bookshelf in half. I must tell you about one of these women because her life truly is a story of accomplishing something significant from nothing, from nearly being homeless to feeding the homeless.

When I lived in Celebration, Florida, I met a very brave woman from Germany, and I watched a transformation take place in her that left me in awe of what a single mother could accomplish. First of all, I must say that she's been one of the humblest people I have ever met, and I believe that is key to her success. She's never been afraid to tell me about her weaknesses. In fact, she is quick to be vulnerable, acknowledging and owning anything she considers to be a weakness, and she remains humble. I can tell you why she is able to do that: she has put her faith in God alone and chosen not to allow bitterness to take root in her. She has a hundred reasons why she could be bitter but she refuses and chooses to give grace instead.

Bettina moved to America to marry a famous wrestler, 2 Cold Scorpio. She became a mother while living in a foreign land, far from family and support. I will let Bettina share her story in her own words, and then I will tell you the amazing details she does not mention.

# Embrace the Journey

———∞———

My name is Bettina Leyla Grzeskowiak, the founder of a nonprofit called Embrace of Celebration. I was born in 1972 and raised in Hanover, Germany. I was married to a professional wrestler, 2 Cold Scorpio. We got separated in 2011, and I raised my son as a single mom without any support, car, or financial help. I came out of my marriage because it was toxic and abusive. It was not easy in a foreign country without any support. All those challenges made me the person I am today. It taught me that no matter how hard life can be, we have to keep going and find solutions to any problems that we face. We grow and learn from the difficulties. Without those challenges, we could not really know how people in bad circumstances feel. Those who go through hard times in life can identify with many others, and that gives us opportunities to support one another and have real compassion and empathy.

All those struggles helped me to identify with many people who go through hard times. I know there is so much I can do; I can plant seeds and multiply. I founded Embrace of Celebration in 2020 in Celebration, Florida, to make sure to walk my talk and be hands on to share my love and compassion and experience with families in need of a support system. We are putting love into action at Embrace of Celebration.

> In this life, we are on a learning journey. Forgiveness is a big part to learn on that journey.

The key is to guard your heart. Have faith. Love. Give grace. Communicate. Realize. And be a part of redemption.

I have learned to guard my heart and notice when people are not on the same path as me; I must give them grace whether they are or not. Life is a battlefield and we are warriors. Keep spreading kindness and love; spread seeds to multiply. Keep going and do not give up. There is so much to give and do, and we can make a positive impact in the lives of others and their environments. Believe in yourself and keep going. Life is a learning journey with ups and downs. If you keep your eyes open and your mind focused and clear of interruption, you will learn and see and walk and put love into action. Focus on your goal in life, not on the things you could get from the path and goals.

God is always in my heart and I talk to Him every day, many, many times. He has guided me since I was very little.

*Bettina Grzeskowiak*

Founder of Embrace of Celebration
www.embraceofcelebration.org

> What is not mentioned is that when Bettina found herself as a single mother with no money and no car, she rode her bicycle—with a vacuum cleaner in one hand—from house to house, seeking cleaning jobs. She started a cleaning business from nothing, and that business became successful. Little by little, she pushed through the hard obstacles.
>
> Years later, she noticed that just outside Celebration was a large homeless community, so Bettina began talking with them and exploring the issues that brought them to the streets. Many were hard-working parents who lived in either tents, hotel rooms, or cars with their small children. Imagine that: children enrolled in school but without an actual home.
>
> Bettina began taking peanut butter sandwiches to these families. She called me one day to ask if I would make twenty peanut butter sandwiches and put them in paper lunch bags. Bill joined me in putting them together and

Bettina picked up the bags after a busy day of cleaning houses. She delivered them to the families. Pretty soon, she was asking others in the neighborhood to participate.

I will never forget riding with her to a rundown, drugged-out, crime-ridden motel where children ran barefoot. When we got out of the van, the children smiled joyously and ran toward her, calling out, "Bettina! Bettina!" The looks on their faces were evidence that she was the highlight of their week. She embraced each one and gave them their weekly bagged lunch with sandwiches, fruit, and healthy snacks. All of this from a woman who still struggled to make ends meet. I was deeply moved.

Within a short time, Bettina did the impossible. She created a nonprofit called Embrace of Celebration, and they currently feed over 3,000 people each month! She has, with the help of volunteers and donations, provided Christmas for the children too. Have you ever seen a teenage boy cry tears over receiving a basketball? I have. And it is beautiful.

Bettina's life is a message of pushing aside our own comforts and problems in order to be a light to lift others in their times of need. She is proof that when everything seems to be falling apart and there's no way out, you can rise from the ashes and build a legacy.

# Mailbox Massacre

### Kerry Walker

This world is filled with women who have defied the odds, shone in the darkness, fallen to their knees, and risen with healing in their wings. Kerry Walker is one of those women. She is a highly talented, dear friend who has a story that would inspire any woman who is in a seemingly impossible situation. Grab a cup of tea and read her story of miracles.

---

The day began like any other and ended in a way we had unfortunately also become all too familiar with. In 2010, I was working in five Indiana Jones shows a day at Disney's Hollywood Studios. During one particular show, another cast member frantically came on stage and whispered to me that I must immediately check my phone as it had been ringing repeatedly. I had multiple missed calls from my youngest daughter, who was ten years old at the time. She was screaming and crying hysterically to the point where I struggled to understand what she was saying.

Her father, now my ex-husband, had picked her up from school and was driving her around. She was able to communicate to me that "Daddy is sleepy! He hit several cars in the school parking lot!" She then said something that would stop me in my tracks and still haunts me to this day. She said,

## Mailbox Massacre

"Mom, Daddy is going toward the lake!" Fearing for the life of my daughter and feeling helpless from so far away, I told her to slap him in his face. While talking to her, assuring she was still safe and trying to coach her through this traumatic event, I was changing clothes and running through Hollywood Studios to get to her. She did indeed slap him, and when she did, he stopped the car. I told her to get out of the car and run. In her innocent loyalty and love for her father, she said in a frightened, sympathetic tone, "But Daddy is still heading to the lake." My only concern was her safety, so I instructed her, "Let him go, start walking away, and do not get in the car if he comes back!"

When I got home, our car that had been involved in this horrific event was parked in the garage. My daughter was at the neighbor's house, safe and sound, while her father was passed out in bed. I called the police and they came to investigate. However, they expressed there was nothing they could do since he was home in bed. Their suggestion was to let him sleep it off.

---

*I felt even more alone, vulnerable, and unprotected following a situation that could have taken the life of my daughter, with no recourse or repercussions for her offender.*

---

This was not the end. About an hour or so later, our doorbell rang. It was Timmy's dad, one of my oldest daughter's friends. In a tone that expressed both frustration and sympathy, he proceeded to say, "Your husband drove over our cement block mailbox. I need your insurance information, and you're going to have to pay for the damage." This was humiliating for all of us but especially for my daughter, who went to school the next day and got made fun of for her dad's reckless actions. The kids all knew and said, "Oh, he's high again." We were all negatively affected by his choices while he suffered no consequence and had no remorse or repentance.

This is just one of many incidents that by the grace of God we have survived, overcome, and ultimately thrived from with great success; all despite living a life of suffering, pain, abuse, and poverty at the hands of their father, my ex-husband. As an infant and toddler, he had a horrific childhood and was then adopted into a household of physical and emotional abuse. His drug of choice was opioids and then Ketamine. His severe addiction and unstable mental condition caused us to live without transportation, groceries, electricity, and money for basic household needs. My ex-husband and I were together since I was twenty-five years old, finally separating in 2015. I was trapped in an emotionally abusive situation with a powerful narcissistic individual who was clinically diagnosed with bipolar disorder, manic disorder, and a traumatic brain injury.

However, through it all, I was a full-time cast member and principal equity actor at Walt Disney World. I have logged over 20,000 hours of live television segments as a product presenter for shopping channels in Italy, France, and Russia, and for *The Home Shopping Network* in the United States.

Both of my daughters are now successful, award-winning adults. My oldest daughter is an ordained minister for a very large, particular denomination and was recognized as the 2024 top children's pastor in that denomination. She currently has over 200 children in her ministry. My youngest daughter is a graduate of the University of Miami, which she attended on a full academic scholarship, double majoring in broadcast journalism and creative writing. She is a College Emmy award winner, recipient of The Edward R. Murrow Scholarship Award for Excellence in College Broadcasting, and the Steven Sotloff Memorial Scholarship Award winner. She is currently a multimedia journalist reporter and weekend anchor for a top network.

# Mailbox Massacre

> My only explanation is that God had a plan
> and His grace, mercy, and protection
> carried us through.

He never left us or forsook us, and every prayer we prayed was heard and answered. Our struggle and tears turned to success and joy. I raised these girls with an optimistic parental approach of faith in Jesus, love for one another, and service to those in even worse circumstances than our own. We never cursed God and were fully aware of the enemy and earthly darkness that contributed to our difficult journey. We lived in a mindset of gratitude, forgiveness, and service. All glory goes to God!

*Kerry Walker*

# The Eye of the Beholder

## Britany Bloom

The next voice you will hear from in this chapter is one I have known from her very start. I held her in my arms the day she was born. I watched her grow up. Britany is my baby sister. I watched her walk down the aisle on her wedding day—a bride beaming with joy, ready to love and be loved. Unfortunately, she stepped into a chapter of life where she was made to feel small, less than, and not enough. The pain of betrayal and oppression brought her to her knees.

Britany is not one to give up. We prayed and prayed and declared. She read every marriage book that was on the market, it seemed. She made changes in her own life, but they were not reciprocated. When it came time to exit the marriage, I witnessed a broken woman who was barely able to breathe, but for the sake of her children, she pressed on and bloomed into a resilient, strong, powerful woman with a vision. And thank God, she now has an incredible man in her life who encourages her on every level. It is an honor to have my little sister share at our roundtable.

—∞—

*To all who have ever been made to feel worthless and unlovable.*

# The Eye of the Beholder

They say beauty is in the eye of the beholder. What do you see when you look at a dandelion? Most people see a weed. A worthless, irritating weed that they spend money, time, and effort on poisoning, pulling, and burning to eradicate it from their lawns. When I look at a dandelion, I see a precious gift with a bright and cheery bow on top, given to us by our Creator. How can one plant be seen so differently by different people?

The difference here is because early on, I took the time to look closely at the dandelion and ask questions, to learn about its nature and purpose for existing, to see all of its qualities and charms. This made me have a love and appreciation for them. Most people do not bother to spend any time looking past their first impressions and so they miss out on a gift.

Did you know that we are capable of often treating God's gifts and blessings as worthless trash that we toss aside or completely crush? We can actually rob ourselves of blessings when we refuse to see past our own selfishness. Here is a little lesson on what lies within dandelions. I hope your eyes will be opened to see them for what they truly are, not just for what your eyes behold.

All the parts of the plant can be used in various ways as herbal remedies, though the roots and leaves are the most commonly used parts, used to treat liver problems. Native Americans, past and present, also boil dandelions in water they then ingest to treat kidney disease, swelling, skin problems, heartburn, and upset stomach. In traditional Chinese medicine, it has been used to treat stomach problems, appendicitis, and breast problems, such as inflammation or lack of milk flow. In Europe, dandelion milk was used as a remedy for fever, boils, eye problems, diabetes, and diarrhea. It is even used for clearer skin:

> Due to its natural magnesium and zinc content and its potential ability to support detoxification,

dandelion is also known as being good for the skin. It can be used topically in applications like tinctures and poultices and many people also take it in capsule or tea form to help support healthy skin. ("dandelion," Wellness Mama, wellnessmama.com)

This is just a small example of what treasures and blessings lie within this gift that most people call worthless and treat as useless, If beauty is in the eye of the beholder, then that means if you see a dandelion and call it trash, it becomes trash. I will let you in on a little secret. God does not make trash, people do!

> Just because your eye may fail to see the beauty, value, and blessing in what God has created does not change that creation's beauty, value, and blessing it possesses. Not one single bit!

As my daughters were growing up, I would often find myself gazing at them in awe of how beautiful and wonderful they were, and I'd become filled with such a sense of wonder and gratitude that I was chosen to be their mother and that I was blessed to be any part of their lives. This was because I saw them for who they were, not for how they served my purposes for their existence. There were several times, that I recall vividly, when I asked my now ex-husband, "Do you ever just look at them and feel so overwhelmingly blessed?" I asked this with a big smile on my face, wanting him to share in the blessings with me, only to be shocked and saddened when he looked blankly at me, like he had no idea what I was talking about, and he just did not answer. It would break my heart, and still does sometimes, that he was not able to see them for who they are and marvel at the beauty of that. I am sharing this only to further my point that beauty is not found in the eye of the beholder.

## The Eye of the Beholder

My ability to see the beauty of who my daughters are does not add or take away from their beauty and value. My ex-husband's inability to see the beauty and value of who they are does not add or take away from it either. They are who they are because beauty is in the eye of their Creator, and He placed it in them. He called them worthy, so not a single human being can add or take away from who they are and what they are worth!

Dear one, if you have struggled with feeling worthless and unlovable, hear this: the same God who made the marvelous dandelions also made you! The same God who placed such powerful gifts and blessings within a simple plant placed the gifts and blessings you have to offer inside you. Nobody, not one single person on this earth, can take any of that away from you!

---
Just because they are blind to who you are does not make you any less of who you are.

---

I am reminded of the joy I felt as a child (and still do) of finding dandelions and making a wish, then blowing the seeds. I am pretty sure all children do this. Maybe this is another reason why God tells us to be childlike. Children seem to have a way of seeing the blessings God has placed within plain sight that we, as adults, often overlook and miss out on. Never forget that you have joy and blessings to offer to those around you, and let your heart be thrilled when those people come along who see you for who you are and are ready to receive the blessings of your presence in their lives. Those people are like gardeners who understand what a dandelion truly is, and they make room to cultivate them in their gardens among all the other valuable plants. Those people are the ones who harvest the blessings that others will miss.

*Britany Bloom*

# Cotton Panties

## Traci Vanderbush

Hello again. Here we are at this roundtable sharing stories of challenges, triumphs, life lessons, and victories. I am glad to be here—where I can let my hair down a bit. Hopefully you won't mind. I mean, being a preacher's wife sometimes comes with societal expectations and perceptions that peg a woman and nail her into a nice little box with barriers. As Danny Silk says, "In church, we expect people to act like they don't poop. Eventually, ole Bessie blows, and it's a real mess." I am not one for pretending to be without flaws, so I pray you can accept some real thoughts from me about menopause. My words may come across as unprofessional, sometimes improper, whimsical, and, yes, just plain silly, but as we sit at this roundtable, can we ponder aspects of life that are oft not spoken of or expressed?

> There are so many things no one ever tells you about.

For example, I think back to when I graduated from high school and my dad had to teach me how to properly count money back to customers. Yes, I knew how to add, subtract, multiply, and divide, but the technique of counting money back was something my educators did not find to be important. There was no practical teaching for daily living. We kept to the textbook and that was that. It was more a matter of passing government tests and not a matter of learning how to actually do life in this world.

It was my dad who taught me to change the oil in the car every 3,000 miles and how to install a water pump, and he enlightened me as to why it is important to change your home air conditioning filters every month, not to mention that you should drain your water heater regularly to avoid corrosion and help your A/C system by pouring vinegar down the drain line once a month.

My mom taught me how to properly wash laundry and dishes. I watched her vacuum, sweep, and mop, keeping a meticulous house despite the fact that she was just a teenager. She may have dropped out of high school to raise me, but I am grateful I had the privilege of sitting on her freshly cleaned carpet while watching Captain Kangaroo and Sesame Street, inhaling the scent of grilled cheese sandwiches that would soon be coming my way. She knew how to make a home because her mother had modeled homemaking so well.

She taught me how to write when all I wanted to do was cry over writing assignments in school. Though she dropped out of high school to stay home with me when I was born, she never lost her love for the education she'd received. I was the child of a hippie belly dancer, yet she made sure I was in church for Sunday School, Vacation Bible School, and all the church services in between. From Jesus to drum circles, from the scriptures to the movement of an ancient dance, she planted in me a desire for faithfulness and falafels. I guess you can say I was well-cultured at a young age.

I am thankful for the lessons I learned. But, you know, fast-forward a bit and you realize there are things no one really talks about, like how after you give birth, your stomach hangs like a deflated balloon for a time. It is quite shocking to look down at your once-attractive belly only to see it crying out for a good ironing. And no one tells you what it is like to have an episiotomy. I mean, you kinda know you might need one to help in the birthing process, but did anyone else have to sit on an inflatable donut after pushing a baby out, or was that just me?

Do they still have those now? I don't even know. It's been thirty years since I gave birth to my first child.

Do you recall the feeling of milk surging into your breasts when the baby cried? That is a pain that man will never know. Rock-solid feeding bottles, filled to the brim, and when the baby does not quite latch on just right, you clench your eyes closed and tighten your jaw for the first part of the feeding to avoid your pain becoming audible. Oh, yeah, did you try lanolin lotion to soothe the cracking? And if you ever had mastitis, you know the bond of motherhood that makes you feel like a warrior, an overcomer. You could pump your fist in the air and belt out, "I survived!"

> There are a lot of things no one tells you because, honestly, some of it is eclipsed by the glory and beauty of the reward on the other side.

But fast-forward several more years into menopause. What about all the little details no one talks about as you enter the phase of life where you are in the middle—the in-between, the place where you are thinking about how to take care of aging parents, while on the other end, you feel the pull to assist your adult children as they face their own challenges in life? And when you hit fifty, you jolt awake with the realization, *Oh, dear God. We don't have any retirement!* How did time go by so quickly? I was twenty-seven just yesterday, driving my two babies around town, running errands, changing diapers, juggling a senior pastorate. How the heck did that even happen?

No one tells you exactly what it means when they say time flies. When your children are little and you are exhausted from lack of sleep, it seems like true rest is a thousand years away, and it is in those moments that no one tells you just how much you need to cherish those times because, seemingly literally, tomorrow you will be kissing your child goodbye as they walk out your door to begin a new chapter. And no one tells you how you will feel when the empty nest suddenly feels empty.

Is there any preparation for living, really? Or do we seriously all have to learn as we go?

Back to menopause. If you scour the internet, you will find jokes about how the word MEN is found in so many things that relate to women's issues: Consider some of these words:

| | |
|---|---|
| woMAN | MENtal Breakdown |
| feMALE | |
| mADAM | MENstrual Cramps |
| MRs. | |
| sHE | MENopause |
| MENtal Illness | GUYnecologist |

And yes, if you want to misspell a word once again, HISterectomy.

Don't worry. I am not anti-man at all. I love, honor, and greatly respect men who are good men, good fathers, faithful, true, genuine, repentant, full-of-love men who use their power for the good of everyone around them. We need men! I am blessed to be married to one of the best guys in the world, and I do not take that lightly. Ladies, we would not be here without men. The roofs we have over our heads were almost all built by men who straddled lumber and pounded nails in both sun and snow. Thank God for them.

But, you know, it is fun to laugh about the fact that we live our lives in many ways serving MEN in the midst of MENstrual cycles, MENtal breakdowns, and MENopause.

Maybe the "pause" in menopause is telling us, "Hey, it is time to pause and take notice of what is going on inside our body. I mean, we've been having sex, carrying babies, pushing out babies, nursing, serving, and making a living in the middle of loving, and, um—note from the uterus and ovaries—we're tired."

---

*I used to think women were being dramatic when they talked about menopause!*

---

In fact, I remember noticing those little kangaroo pouches that were beginning to show on the bellies of mothers around me and I thought to myself, *Yikes! I'll never let that happen to me.* Yes, I know—naive, naive, naive. It turns out it is not a matter of refusing donuts. It is a matter of hormones that decide to shift and holler "Let's hold on to that fat! We just might need it for protective padding in the future when we fall down."

Perhaps some ladies get to skate through the inevitable transition, but as for myself, I ended up in the emergency room thinking I was having a heart attack. Everything just felt utterly wrong, and, of course, it all had to happen during a historic pandemic. Great timing! Have you ever been awakened by a furnace inside your body that decided to erupt like a volcano? Sweaty sheets are just the most romantic thing. And it is no longer romance that gives you heart palpitations, it is hormones. After my emergency room visit, I did a lot of googling to find out why I felt like a nutcase, and I found I was not alone. In fact, the light of heaven enveloped me when I read that Oprah Winfrey thought she was having a cardiac incident but found out it was menopause. I was not alone! But I still needed answers.

Not only was I experiencing a total body freak out, but I was also experiencing it all while being on the road nearly full time, ministering in seventy-eight different locations during 2023. Planes, trains, automobiles, crowded airports, delays, lost luggage, sleeping in different hotel rooms and host homes (if you are one of the host homes, please know you were a sweet moment of refuge for a woman in distress), jumping time zones, and waking up to use the bathroom in the night only to walk into a hotel closet. A couple of times, I had to open the curtains to peer out the window to remember where I was. "Father, help me," I'd pray. One time, in the middle of a stressful trip, I was working the resource table at my husband's conference and a dear, well-meaning woman came up to me and said, "You're so lucky to live this kind of life. It's like you're on vacation *all the time!*" I felt a fire rise up within me, and this time, it wasn't a hot flash. But I smiled and said, "Yes, it's quite amazing." Then I went into a bathroom stall and cried.

You might say, "But where is the great woman of faith? You're supposed to be Superwoman, fueled by the Holy Ghost!" Oh, I am here all right. Full-on here and full of faith, but even as we walk the path of righteousness, it is not guaranteed that we won't walk through valleys. Yet God is faithful to walk with us through them and help us to discover what we need to know for such a time as this.

Recently, several of my close friends got together and discussed these life changes: why were urinary tract infections suddenly a thing? And yeast infections? Weight gain? And just plain feeling like we might need to check ourselves in for a mental evaluation? We talked about developing a Zoom meeting for ladies to gather and share the latest, greatest solutions they have come across to survive this time of life. If you're in that season and you've been searching online for solutions, you're probably familiar with words like "cranberry." By the way, have you tasted pure, 100 percent cranberry juice? If not, be sure to film yourself while trying it. It is probably best not to try it in a church service because your facial contortions might be mistaken for demonic possession. Anyway, back to the words: D-mannose, lubricant, estrogen, St. John's Wort, flaxseed, black cohosh, exercise, breathing techniques, hormone replacement therapy, and more! All of that to say, the group of ladies I was speaking with seemed excited and relieved to find they were not alone. We found community, connection, and inspiration simply by being vulnerable enough to speak of the things no one ever told us about.

Speaking of the "no one ever tells you" category again, I was never told, until a couple of weeks ago, that I would need to change my undergarment selection. My delightful lady doctor smiled as she informed me that the underwear I have come to love could be a problem. Now, let me first say, she said, "Absolutely no thongs," and I was glad to hear that because I have never been a fan of wedgies. So that wasn't an issue for me. The doctor prescribed a shopping spree for new panties. I am not talking about Victoria's Secret or some other place with things to make you feel attractive. I am talking about a shopping spree for good old-fashioned cotton panties. Everything else must go. But what about no-show undies, seamless ones that are cut just right for certain outfits? Would cotton provide me with the right fit? And would it make me the bearer of bad panty lines?

I scoured the internet for the best-rated cotton panties, but it was overwhelming and too confusing. I cannot order undergarments to try on and then send them back. So I went to a place I would prefer not to go. Walmart—because I did not want to spend loads of money on something I wasn't certain would be the answer. After thirty minutes of staring at multiple packages of panties in Walmart's lingerie department, I finally decided to consult God. Now was the time for prophetic insight and a word of knowledge. "Father, which ones should I choose?" With war and disease going on in this world, how did the search for cotton panties become an issue of prayer? God forgive me. Why did this seem like such a big deal? Perhaps because everything that goes along with menopause is magnified, and it seems like a massively big deal.

After deciding to instead spend my prayers on the sick, the captives, and the homeless, I simply grabbed the closest Fruit of the Looms, and they actually have not disappointed. They will do for now. The good news is that not all cotton panties have to look like my grandmother's underwear, and gratitude has filled my heart for the magic of puffy cotton balls that grow on plants. How did I forget the childlike wonder of driving past fields that appeared to be speckled with snow, bearing softness that could be plucked away and turned into beautiful apparel and coverings that bring warmth? And that right there is where the doctor's prescription turned into something wonderful: cotton panties restored to me the joy of cotton.

That brings me to this question: in your own life, is there joy that's been lost along the way? Is there a simplistic piece of wonder, a sliver of happiness that seems to have dissolved under the weight of living in the day-to-day challenges of this world? What's been getting your cotton panties in a wad?

---

*Breathe, step back, take a look at your situation, and find something beautiful in it. Relish that thing!*

---

When hormones try to convince you there's no light at the end of the tunnel, refuse to live in that place the author of Lamentations did, who wrote, "My soul is bereft of peace; I have forgotten what happiness is" (Lamentations 3:17 ESV). Instead, we have the promise that sorrows and suffering will pass and joy is our inheritance. We may weep in the night, but joy comes in the morning. More than mere happiness, which is temporary, joy is full, complete, and eternal. The fullness of joy is found in the presence of the Lord. So no matter what "they" never told you, we are held by the One who made our magnificent human-bearing bodies of wonder. The Maker of cotton knows just what we need. And that is enough to get us through.

*Traci Vanderbush*

# The Knowing

### Robin Hertz Hempel

We women carry a special intuition. I believe it is because the Comforter, the Holy Spirit, who acts as teacher and guide, is woven into our DNA from the very start. He knew us and formed us from before the foundation of the world, according to Scripture. Most women are naturally nurturers and guides. As we lean into the Father, we experience His different gifts. He speaks to us in many ways. Whether it is words of knowledge, prophecy, wisdom, etcetera, there is an innate deeper knowing within each of us.

My precious and incredibly life-giving friend Robin shares an experience in which listening to this "knowing" brought her through a life-versus-death situation. Her story is a reminder to listen to the One who leads you and tune out the voices of others who, even though they mean well, may not understand what God is telling you to do. On this journey of life, we must live by every word that comes from His mouth.

―∞―

Throughout life, I slowly learned to trust my "knowings." When doubts crept in, something always happened that reminded me I had to trust. I believe we can hear from God and have that "knowing" deep inside. I want to tell you about the moment that convinced me to never let anyone talk me out of my knowing.

I was going through my divorce when our yearly friends' snowboard-ski trip came up. My soon-to-be ex, Don, told me to

# The Knowing

take the kids and he would pay for it. We always went with our friends Joe and Lorraine, who had kids around the same ages as ours. My son, Grant, was eleven and my daughter, Audrey, was eight. Something inside every fiber of my being did not want to go on this trip. I tried canceling the tickets, and I even got physically sick.

> I told Don and Lorraine I felt like we shouldn't go, but they all pushed and pressed me to go.

I reluctantly gave in and we all went to Aspen. Grant got sick on the airplane, and he never got sick while traveling. I was edgy but settled in. Everything was great until the last day of skiing, when I called Lorraine and asked if we could all go to a different mountain and ski there for the day. She said the kids wanted to go back to an area called Crazy Train. This was the problem. My gut and my knowing were *Do not go to the Crazy Train area.* That was the exact place I knew we shouldn't ski. Instead of being strong enough and forcing the issue, I let her talk me into it. I relented and went along with the plan. *Breathe, Robin. You're being ridiculous. Everything is going to be okay.* I tried to convince myself that my nagging "knowing" intuition was deceiving me.

Everyone was excited about the adventure. All seemed well except Audrey kept falling, so she and I lagged behind everyone else. Audrey and I ended up going down an easier slope, but when we got to the bottom, no one was there. Finally, I could see Grant and the gang slowly trickling down the mountain toward us. As thankful as I was seeing them all snowboarding and skiing down, I knew something had happened.

Lorraine's first words to me were, "Thank God you didn't see what happened to Grant." Grant was snowboarding on one of the hills on the Crazy Train terrain that turned out not to be a hill at all but a jump! And a high one at that. He fell right down the middle and landed flat on his back. "Basically like a rag doll," Lorraine expressed to me. Thank God he was wearing a helmet and CamelBak, and it protected his head and spine. That was the first year it was mandatory for children to wear helmets. The fall was so high and severe that they had the medics come check to make sure he did not break anything. Surprisingly, Grant felt good enough to snowboard down himself.

I thought, *Hum, that sounded pretty bad.* However, my higher self said, "Let's go get checked out." We went to the local Aspen hospital around 4:00 p.m. They did a CT scan and x-rays. The ER doctor said, "Thank goodness he didn't break anything." I was told we should expect him to be in pain since he'd had a big fall, and to give him Tylenol or Motrin. The doctor said if he developed red line bruises or welts to bring him back immediately.

We settled in at the condo and I began making dinner with both families. So fun! The kids were all hanging out and watching television.

> Out of nowhere, something came over me and I "knew" I had to take Grant back to the hospital.

He was not in pain and his cheeks were pink from spring skiing. He looked so healthy and fine. The only thing that was different was his shoulder was achy. No red lines, but I just "knew." I couldn't shake the feeling! I watched my son as he was hanging out with his friends, watching television, seeming to be perfectly normal. But when God takes over, the nag is different. I actually felt something come over me that put me into action mode. "Lorraine, I am taking Grant back to the hospital," I said. She thought I should just wait until the morning, especially since there was a snowstorm and it was already 9 o'clock at night. This is when that "bigger than me" thing took over. *Yes.* It was bigger and more powerful than me.

# The Knowing

I actually remember clocking the feeling. I did not care. I knew I was taking him back no matter what anyone said. So off we went.

We made our way down the mountains through the nighttime darkness, beautiful snowflakes, and low visibility. Calling the hospital from the car, I explained, "My eleven-year-old son was there earlier today and I'm bringing him back. I know you missed something and I need you to do whatever it takes to check his internal organs, like his spleen." I actually used the exact word "spleen." The words rolled in through the top of my head and out of my mouth with no thought process from me. It was an illogical feeling but a command to me to make sure I said it so it was heard. When we got there, they were ready for us with a child IV specialist for the MRI with contrast. Quickly, the results were back, and the same ER doctor who was there earlier took me over to the scans and said, "Do you see this dark mass on the MRI? Well, that is blood. When the surgeon comes in, he will explain more." *Whoa! The surgeon?* That threw me a little. This was getting real quickly.

A Dr. Rodman then showed up in full scrubs, ready for surgery. He was even wearing a hat and facemask. He was ready. I was not. He took me over to see the scans again and told me that my son needed "emergency life-saving surgery." Grant had split his spleen open and was bleeding internally, and there was zero way it was stopping on its own. His perfect little body was in trouble. I thought, *Wait! What just happened?* Honestly, I was suddenly in shock and needed to regroup and talk with Grant. We prayed together and I promised him he would be okay. I called his dad and told him he needed to fly to Aspen because Grant was headed in for emergency surgery.

You know those old little flip phones? I remember as I was allowing my son, my love of my life to be wheeled away on the gurney and cut open for surgery, I opened my flip phone and there it was: 11:11 p.m., and I knew he would be okay. 11:11.

Those are our special numbers. As they took Grant down the hall to the operating room, I pulled the doctor aside and asked him to do whatever he needed to repair Grant's spleen and save it. Again, out of my mouth came important information. Forty minutes later, Dr. Rodman came out with a huge smile on his face, saying the split was millimeters away from a main artery and he was able to put a mesh around the spleen and save it.

Three days after the surgery, as I was roaming around the hospital floors in the middle of the night, I ran into the surgeon again. He pulled me aside, looked deep into my soul, and told me that if I had not brought Grant back to the hospital that night, he most likely would not have woken up or we would have had to fly him to Denver, and it would have been a totally different story. I could have found my son gone in the morning. Thank You, God, for speaking so loudly to me! Thank You.

> I cannot be grateful enough for higher guidance and for the Holy Spirit taking over!

And thank God I listened and allowed myself to get out of ego and pride and acted on the knowing He gave me. Knowings and acting on them saved my son's life!

Robin Hertz Hempel

# From Addiction to Freedom

## Celeste Keplin-Weeks

In this life, God often brings people across our paths who stir the heart and spirit at the very roots of what we know to be true. Their ability to convey what we feel on a profound level makes it seem almost as if they can read our minds. That's how it was when Celeste Keplin-Weeks came into my life. The funny thing is that I can't fully recall how we found each other, but her online writing impacted me deeply, and that's where our journey together began.

Celeste is a Spirit-filled Christian Cree Native who overcame major obstacles and decided to pursue writing to bring life to others. Around the time that she and I "met" via the internet, I joined a writing school called Story Summit. It was there that I learned screenplay writing and entered a couple of mentorships with award-winning film writers, and let me tell you, I often felt like a complete imposter. I've always had a burning passion for writing, but I nearly allowed my fears and self-doubts to talk me out of stepping forward in that gift, but God!

Just as I was feeling I should bow out of the school, God woke me up with the words "Santa Fe" in my mind. I had never been to Santa Fe or even given it a thought. Continually, those words kept appearing, so I told my husband, "Maybe a revival is coming to Santa Fe. I don't know what it is, but I know I'm supposed to pay attention." A couple of weeks later, my mentor said there would be a women-only writers' event in Santa Fe! Needless to say, I signed up immediately.

As the event drew closer, the organizers announced that there were scholarships for people of other cultures. At that moment, the beautiful writings of Celeste came to my mind, so I contacted her about applying. Long story short, she and I got to spend a mind-blowing few days with highly talented people while we engaged in releasing the God-given gift within. Our work was heard and read by people of note, and that's something we will never forget. She was invited to share her poetry from the platform. The feeling in the room was thick, tangible, and powerful. I'm truly honored to have Celeste share a bit of her story with you, and I pray you can feel what we felt in the room that night.

Back in my "drunken fool" days as the happy little lush of the family, my sister wrote a letter to me in response to the meager requests I had made on my Christmas wish list. "Low Expectations!" was her opening statement. Within her letter, she gently chided me for not desiring nor giving much in life. She gave me four different versions of Jeremiah 29:11.

---
She knew my heart, you see.
---

She knew I had been living heart-wrecked from being denied children and in losing my husband, a sorrow that had shadowed me since his passing over twenty years prior. These were my sorrows I dwelled in. But in reading that, a spark was ignited. It felt like maybe God still cared for me, that He wanted me to get out of this life of drinking and little else, even to become worthwhile as a person. *Could He still have a use for me?* I kept the idea in my heart and treasured it.

My personal idea of God was more than a little skewed. I was born into a Cree Indigenous family of the Turtle Mountain Band of Chippewa Cree Tribe of North Dakota, the first daughter of four children, between two brothers. Our tribe was steeped in the Catholic faith. My family lived an off-reservation life in Spokane, Washington, with that religious tradition intact.

I and my brothers went to the sophisticated St. Charles Parish School. Its campus had sparkling water fountains, and life-size alabaster statues of the saints all through the buildings. The church itself was a curved geometrical architectural structure; its ceiling and walls featured glowing art deco, its windows stained-glass biblical scenes. And, of course, there were the stately dressed clergy and nuns and all the classy parishioners. This was altogether beyond anything my parents could have dreamed of. My mother had attended a one-room schoolhouse, and my father had been taken to a faraway Indian boarding school, a place where discipline and life were often atrociously cruel.

My religious upbringing gave me a powerful sense of right and wrong. I understood that those Ten Commandments meant that life was a matter of doing the right thing; also, they seemed to indicate that God was the scorekeeper. My takeaway was that the system of admitting sins in a private little confessional booth to the priest decreased a tally of wrongs, and performing the penance he indicated would increase my score to the good. And that was "the all" of my understanding from religious school. Obviously, there was much more, but I was a daydreamy kid. The religious instruction did not have the sweet appeal for my good behavior as did the Easter Bunny, the tooth fairy, and jolly old St. Nicholas, who watched over me—with his gifts in mind—to see if I had been a good girl.

Overall, my parents provided a good home, yet none of us seemed to hold any substantial relational connection to one another beyond sharing the same house. When our parents spoke to us, it was nearly always to scold, reminding us of our strict rules. To avoid severe punishment, we younger ones were to honor those rules. The dire punishment was my father's belt, strapping us as hard and as long as he could. The rage and hate in his face were more fearful than the whippings. When he strapped me and my cries subsided, we avoided one another for days, or until the next time I misbehaved.

In these last few years, the Indian boarding school abuses have been revealed.

---
> I now understand what my father experienced, how he had been indoctrinated into reacting with rage over the misbehavior of his children.
---

Like many, he had no love in his upbringing, only anger or indifference, and he was incapable of showing his own children any love. But God had plans for this family.

When I was a young teen, my indifference to religious faith and my family became solid. I had begun to stray from home for days, even weeks, despite the beatings. But then my parents were invited to a Pentecostal prayer group. Soon they both made the decision to become born again followers of Jesus. The physical and verbal abuse stopped. Instead, they prayed for me. I thought I had "won." I was able to come and go as I pleased. I was disdainful of their godly witnessing attempts. I only wanted to go stepping out with my girlfriends, seeking parties and handsome older guys who thrilled us. I wanted to party and have fun. I wanted to find a nice guy who would love me.

Then at age sixteen, I married a popular guy who was the life of the party. The party never ended, but the marriage did after seven years. In that time, I learned that I could not bear children. I'd done away with the wild party life, but there would be no family of my own. I reunited with my parents and the Lord in a good way, and when I was twenty-five, the most goodhearted man of the Klamath Tribe of Oregon found me. All through our marriage, we were kindred souls. He was tenderhearted, as I was, but strong where I was insecure. He said I gave him courage. We both loved God. I was living whole and blessed. And then after seven years, my husband was killed by a drunk driver.

Just as I did as a child when punishment came at me, I disengaged and drifted alone. After spontaneously accepting some wine at an office after-work gathering, I found that having some drinks brought me out of the deadness. I talked and joked easily, just the way I had with my husband. I liked myself when I was drinking. I was alive again. I found a whole lot of people who liked me too. I was enchanted with how alcohol made me feel, even when occasional hangovers started, and those times when I became embarrassingly drunk, I laughed them off with my friends and convinced myself that all was well.

Many years went by. I could tell you about being a "functioning" alcoholic, and even of extended periods of living clear of drinking, just as my father did. Still, the lighthearted feelings that drinking gave me *always stayed* in the periphery of my awareness. Addiction was like the most delightful love relationship that slowly goes horribly wrong. I found myself suffering constantly, comforted only with some of the more potent drink, just like a bit of attention from a desperately desired one. I knew this way of life was warped and wrong, but when gathering with friends to share drinks and conversation, I felt good about myself, valued. We talked about everything except our common addiction, of course, only laughing off the hangovers, slurred speech, tripping over "air." Soon I longed for it day and night, even when I was no longer soothed and the physical anguish was eased only a bit. But then came Jeremiah 29:11.

I felt I owed God a turnaround. I knew I had to make myself straighten up so that I could resume that scoreboard of good behavior marks and get good enough for God to notice and bless me. One day, in the winter following my sister's eye-opening letter to me, I slipped on the porch ice and badly hurt myself. I called a nearby drinking crony to come help me, asking him to let me stay at his home for a few days until the worst of the sprain or strain eased up. I would give him money to get vodka and cigarettes to help me with the pain but he would return hours later with what I needed mostly gone. Even in my excruciating pain, he attempted sexual advances as I lay broken on his sofa.

One night, I was dozing on that sofa, trying to sleep through the agony, when I "felt" God deep in my spirit asking me, "Have you had enough?" There was light and love in the question. Immediately I cried out my *yes* in the same way, inside my spirit. Instantly, I felt the spirit of addiction leave as though it were "pulled" out. Suddenly I was clean and free. The morning dawn had come as well, and in a new feeling of confident strength, I demanded to be brought back to my home. That man quickly and wordlessly complied.

It turned out that I had a fractured hip, and even through the surgical implant of a pin and the weeks of healing time, I was in awe of the God who heals, Jehovah Rapha. I spent that healing time soaking in His Word, loving the God who had done this for me without my working to become worthy of His favor. Most of my life I had surrounded myself with barriers against my misery from physical abuse, life sorrows, and grief yet still living focused on my anguish. And now, nearly ten years later, I live forever free of that anguish of being mistreated, lonely, and deeply addicted. The rescue I needed was through the faithful prayers of my family that were answered by a loving God.

If there is someone in your life who is suffering from addiction or deep sorrows, do not give up on them. Make time for fervent prayer each time God brings them to mind. Amazing grace is on the way.

> "'I know the plans and thoughts that I have for you,' says the LORD, 'plans for peace and well-being and not for disaster, to give you a future and a hope.'" (Jeremiah 29:11 AMP)

*Celeste Keplin-Weeks*

Spirit-filled, Christian Cree Native
Award-winning writer

# Dismantling Panic

## Cheryl Ricker

I have the privilege of knowing many incredible women. They each carry a special gift. One of the rarest gifts is one of childlikeness wrapped in wisdom and knowledge. My friend Cheryl Ricker is one who is clothed in such a way. Cheryl is, in her words, a Jesus lover, wife, mother, intercessor, artist, author, ghostwriter, screenwriter, speaker, LifeWave brand partner, and agent and literary manager at her literary agency, Dunamis Words. But if you ever have the chance to experience her laughter and the oceans of blue, delight-filled joy that stream from her eyes, then you have been in the presence of a joy that's been formed in fires you would never imagine. And that is why I am happy to bring her to our virtual roundtable to share a beautiful life lesson.

———∞———

Dwight and I thought nothing of it when we sat on a wide stone ledge in Jerusalem to rest our tired legs and share a romantic moment … until an unleashed big black dog came lunging toward us.

"Nooo!" screamed the owner, chasing after him from several feet behind.

"I'll protect you," Dwight announced, flinging his big wide arm around me so fast that *bam*—he knocked us both backward and upside down, off the ledge's six-foot drop, into a prickly bush below!

It might not have been as bad if Dwight had landed beside me, but no, his big body had to come crashing down flat on top

## Dismantling Panic

of me, flattening every little part of me, including my poor little, not-so-full-anymore bladder!

Cujo's mom leaned over the ledge's drop panting. "You okay?"

"Yeah, we're fine," said Dwight, moaning.

I shot him a look. "Speak for yourself. You had a cushy landing pad!"

Reaching for me with fresh, glassy-eyed concern, he gathered me into his strong, steady arms and slowly helped me to my feet. "I'm so sorry," he said. "You okay? I feel terrible."

I sighed. "You feel terrible? I feel terrible too." I finally managed a smile as we held a gaze. "Love you."

As much as I hated this painful experience, it became a good-bad dog metaphor in our marriage about how fear and panic cause us to overcompensate and make bad situations worse.

I used to be a pro at this when learning to drive. If I perceived a car coming slightly over its lane into mine, I would jerk my wheel away (yikes!) rather than stay in control and carefully maneuver with the right balance. It is because of God's grace I stayed in one piece! That and the fact my mom hardly ever let me drive.

We overreact relationally when others hurt us. We tend to act according to the flesh and hurt them even more rather than bless them in return or respond according to Holy Spirit's fruit of love, joy, peace, patience, goodness, kindness, gentleness, and self-control.

I battle a disease called cervical dystonia, a painful movement disorder where my neck moves in involuntary, funky ways and fails to turn when I want it to turn. Fear and panic, with all its muscle-kicking-into-action adrenaline, sadly over-fuels dystonia. But that is not the biggest reason why I have learned to throw off fear and panic and instead put on Christ and His supernatural ways. It is out of my love for Christ that I choose to trust and obey and say yes to my reliable Savior who calls us to peace and rest.

When Christ calls us to something, He empowers us to succeed. He extends an invitation to the perfect, peaceful covering of His strong, steady arm which is always ready to stabilize us on every limb or ledge—safe and secure from the "big black dog" and every one of his ferocious attacks.

Instead of focusing on who or what we are running from, we must fix our eyes on the One we run to and run with. That is our big-smiling, worry-free Jesus. When we sink our trust in Him and His goodness, we are never put to shame.

> "Some trust in chariots and some in horses, but we trust in the name of the LORD our God." (Psalm 20:7 ESV)

*Cheryl Ricker*

www.cherylricker.com
Facebook: Cheryl Ann Ricker

# Who Am I?

### Libby Higgins

This table is proving to be enlightening and awe-inspiring as everyone shares their story. I have known many of these ladies for years, but there's so much I did not know about their backgrounds, their stories of walking through the fire, and their arrivals at this table to share what they learned. As I read the following story, I felt my love and appreciation grow for Libby Higgins. I knew part of the battle she endured, but I did not know the half of it!

---

It was 2011 and I was a stay-at-home mom of two little girls ages six and three. All I had ever wanted to do in life was have babies and be present to watch them grow up. My daughters were my world. I was married to my high school sweetheart, and we had been together for sixteen years in total. I had recently pursued a "hobby job" of being a yoga instructor, which I loved doing. I was the worship leader at our church, of which my dad was the pastor. I had friends, I exercised regularly, I was a part of a lovely community. From the outside, my life was everything it was meant to be.

My husband was the youth pastor at our church. He was also in college, studying to be an art teacher, as part of an occupational retraining program since he had injured his back in his previous construction career. He loved our girls and was very invested in their lives. He was charismatic and creative. He had friends and hobbies. He was close to his family. From the outside he was everything he was meant to be. The only "thing" was that he was abusive to me. Physical, mental, emotional, sexual abuse, and pornography, were significant parts of our marriage which began the month after we said I do.

I was raised in a pastor's home and believed firmly in "till death do us part." I was a virgin on our wedding day and had done everything *right* to get myself to this place in life! Every time the abuse occurred, my husband would become very apologetic and self-deprecating.

> And in order to be the "good Christian wife," I believed I was supposed to be, it was my responsibility to forgive him and to conceal his transgression by not telling others about it.

I fully believed that we would work through our issues, God would help us, he would change, we would heal, and we would be able to be together forever. I told no one about what was happening at home. Not my friends, not my family, no one. After all, what would people think? The youth pastor? Abuse and pornography? It would have been devastating for him to have other people know. The reality would have hit like a shock wave! I was committed to being a faithful wife, and I was very scared of what people would think, so I told no one. As a result, I was stuck in an unending cycle of abuse. I felt trapped. I felt hopeless. I felt despair.

In August of 2011, after a particularly horrible situation of mental manipulation and emotional abuse, I had had enough. My misery finally outweighed my fear and I announced to my husband that I was separating from him. (As a sidenote: the mental and emotional abuse was and has been far more sinister and challenging to heal from than anything else. At least when the abuse was physical, my pain felt legitimized. Please know that if you are suffering from or recovering from this type of abuse, your pain and confusion are real. You are not alone.)

## Who Am I?

What I wanted from a separation was for us to get help, to go to counseling (again), and to repair our marriage. That did not happen. Instead, my husband refused to go with me to counseling, and he made fun of me for making "such a big deal" over it all.

In October 2011 I moved out. I lived on my best friend's couch with nothing but what was in my backpack for eighty-seven days. I saw my girls several days each week. I started working as many hours as I could at the local gym, where I had been teaching yoga. I was dancing on the very fragile line of being suicidal. I started going to therapy once a week and began the rebuilding process.

In one of my counseling sessions, my therapist asked me "Who are you?" Dutifully, I listed all of my titles: I am a mother, a wife, a worship leader, a daughter, a friend, a teacher.

> He lovingly said to me, "Those are all of the things you *do*, but who are you *really*? Who does God say you are? Why did He make you?"

I was thirty-four years old. I had been raised in the Christian faith. I accepted Jesus into my heart at the age of three and had served in the church for my entire life. I loved Jesus and was fully committed to saying yes to whatever I felt Him calling me to do. But in that moment, sitting with my counselor, I literally had no answer to the question of why God made *me*? I was silent. I was stunned. I was dumbfounded. I was embarrassed. I was a tearful and sobbing mess. The truth was, I had no idea who I was.

Over the next two years, I sat in that same office once a week with the therapist to whom I literally owe my life, and the answer to that question slowly began to unfold. I began to discover a love, acceptance, and grace for myself that I had never known. I discovered ugly truths about why and how I had found myself in a sixteen-year abusive relationship. I sat with that counselor during weeks when I had spent too much time drinking and going out on dates with other men who had nefarious ambitions. I began to discover my strengths, my voice, my courage and, most importantly, I started to realize that I was, and am, a daughter of the Most High God! And because of that, I am deeply loved no matter what I do.

During those two years, my marriage came to an end in divorce. I went from being a stay-at-home mom to only seeing my girls half the time and working lots of hours just to make ends meet. Yet through it all, I felt the truest joy and contentment ever in experiencing Jesus as close to me as my next breath. Psalm 34:18 says that He is near to the brokenhearted, and I found that to be so very true.

Slowly (and yet also quickly!) my life began to be rebuilt. I would have been happily content to be a single mom for the rest of my life. Yet, just like so many other things, God knew what I needed more than I could have known. I am now married to an amazingly strong Christian man, and together we have two more children. We now also have a grandson on the way! We are graced to live a full and rewarding life. We are far from perfect, and I am quite happy to tell everyone about it!

I no longer feel like I am hiding in plain sight. I live with honesty and vulnerability, deeply rooted in knowing that, as a daughter of the Most High King, His love far exceeds any other challenge that comes my way in life, and that no matter where I go or what happens to me in the process, He is good, faithful, and trustworthy. And me? I am His kiddo. End of story.

*Libby Higgins*

Pastor, Living Word Chapel, Glenwood City, Wisconsin
www.livingwordchapel.com

# Hot Mess to Destiny

## Amber Twigg

We women too often talk ourselves out of pursuing the dreams in our hearts because of the current hot mess we see in the mirror. If this is you, know there is beauty, fire, and promise wrapped up in that image you see in the mirror! Everything around you may seem messy and out of order, or you might feel that your back is against a wall, but God creates beautiful mosaics of life and color out of your broken little pieces. He is the master artist, brilliant with your shards and tattered bits. My friend Amber found a faithful friend in Jesus, who walked her into her destiny despite impossibilities, and she has become a powerful, insightful minister. Amber has a message for you today.

—∞—

How do you go from being a hot mess to a burning torch for the Lord? I am glad you asked. Well, you did not ask, but you are reading this right now and I believe this is a God setup. Let's understand that this is a divine moment for you because the words you are about to read will inspire the life you were always meant for, the Christ life. But before we get into what you were always meant for, let's address what you were *not* meant for. You were never meant for rejection, self-hatred, or criticism. You were never meant for low-level thinking. You were never meant for hopelessness or depression. You were never meant to be left at the mercy of others, waiting on them to determine whether you were valuable or not. You were meant for the glory of God.

Thank God all this other stuff feels so terrible because if any of that stuff felt awesome, you would live in it. Jesus came to rescue you from this. That's what He did for me and that is what He will do for you. He will continue to do it for you. You see, from the moment you were born, the seduction and temptation to be persuaded to gain the world's acceptance has always been lurking in people's ears. Humanity has been selling out its God-given birthright for mankind's approval since the days of Adam and Eve.

I, just like you, bought the lie that I needed the acceptance of others to make me feel valued. How much of a lie that was. This makes me mad just thinking about it. Such a waste of life living low-level at the mercy of the liar. I am clenching my fist just thinking about all the years I wasted on low-level living when I was meant to display the astonishing glory and truth of the Lord Jesus Christ. I am writing this so you never spend any of your days living low-level at the mercy of the world's value system that only brings about shame, regret, and torment.

The hamster wheel of striving for false perfection is dangled in front of every human, and they eagerly enter into the treacherous game of man-pleasing. However, Jesus is the game changer; He eradicated the game. Christ annihilated the addiction of approval for me and gave me His life. That's what He will do for you too. See, Jesus not only removed my old, decaying life, but He also gave me new life. He gave me His very own life, the life of God. And He will do the same for you. He gives you His very own life. This, my friend, gives you insurmountable satisfaction that just grows every moment, every day, and every hour. The light of knowing Him gets brighter and brighter. The world and its clutches will lose its grip on your mind and life. Coming into Christ makes you wonder why you ever even participated in the things that lead to shame.

I am so fascinated by Christ and His indwelling presence and how the Lord constantly pulls us into all that He is. Christ restores our mind and our love and gives us hope in Him. I wish I knew back then that knowing Jesus would change my perspective into His perspective and that just by default, my emotions and feelings would come into alignment with all the Lord is. That is what is available to you too. And I believe, as you are reading this, you are feeling a fresh desire to intimately love the new life Christ has for you, and that you will get invigorated by the Holy Spirit, day by day, moment by moment. I am trusting the Lord to pull you into everything He is and that your life will reflect the glory of the Lord. It is what you are always destined for. So go ahead, be all that Christ called you to be. It is your best life ever. It is the one you were meant for. It is the one in which purpose is found, destiny is found, and where regrets will never beat you down ever again. It is the life lived in love in the presence of God, where no shame or condemnation can ever eat your life up again.

This is the life of Christ, and His life is your very own life. So go ahead and be all that Christ is. You have full permission. It was given to you the moment Christ gave you His life on the cross.

## Amber Twigg

Founder and Director of Amber Twigg Ministries
https://ambertwigg.com

# Happiness Indeed

## Sally Hanan

Many years ago, Bill and I were working with a school of ministry in Austin, Texas. The school met in multiple locations around the city, and one of those locations in particular brought us across the coolest, wittiest, and most brilliant Irish couple. Sally and Gerry Hanan have been in our lives ever since. Not only are their words of wisdom and humor life-giving, but the sounds of their voices flow like a healing balm to the listener.

I've witnessed Sally's life through the ups and downs, the trials and triumphs, and I can say that even in the middle of grief, she has a way of smiling and turning her affection to the Father. Her ability to do so opens the windows of heaven to where rivers of freedom move into the people around her. I also believe her heart posture is one reason that the Holy Spirit has given her brilliant solutions to walk people into wholeness. If you've ever sought Christian counseling but it wasn't quite enough to fix the triggers, I highly recommend you purchase her books: *Fix Yourself in Jesus*, *Empower Yourself in the Holy Spirit*, and *Coach Yourself with the Father*.

In fact, this book you're reading right now would not exist without Sally. I'm so thankful for being a recipient of her gifts and talents but especially of her kindness. I'm thrilled to invite you into Sally's story so you can learn how she found happiness when she felt she wasn't enough.

# Happiness Indeed

My four nights of night shift were over. My sleep was very much enjoyed. And now I was alone in our flat in Dublin, Ireland, with the dulled sounds of the city suburbs moving around the walls that protected the tiny patch of grass, and my washing on the line, three floors down.

I leaned back into our ratty armchair while lax evening light napped in long squares on the carpet and let silent tears fall. I felt like a total failure. I'd only wanted to be a nurse because I couldn't think of anything else to do. An English and history lover in high school, no career seemed to appeal. All I knew was that I didn't want to sit in a classroom for another three years, and back in those days in Ireland, a young woman could get a nursing degree and a salary by working and taking eight weeks of classes a year for three years. Deal.

I took off after school to live a little first, settling into Andalusian life with a host family and learning Spanish as quickly as I could, while providing many laughs as I stumbled over similar words like *pollo* and *polla*. I chased boys, organized drinking parties, avoided anything that looked like responsibility, and came back to Ireland ripe as a cocoa bean and ready to be a great nurse.

Only I wasn't. I couldn't get my mind around the body parts and chemistry of drugs, couldn't work quickly, couldn't multitask, couldn't look busy doing nothing. The only thing I felt comfortable doing was talking to patients, listening, explaining, understanding. I can't count how many people I forgot about on the commode, or women I left stripped to the waist behind flimsy curtains. Or how late I started the observation round. Or how I froze when someone had a heart attack.

Fortunately, student nurses are just that—students, so someone was always ready to rush in and fix my inability to just "get it" already, "do it right" already. But it wasn't just that. I felt completely inadequate. I wasn't good enough, clever enough, likeable enough. I wasn't enough at all. And so there I sat in the twilight feeling sorry for myself when truth dropped into my heart almost as audibly as a living voice. "Even if you sit here for the rest of your life, you are still enough."

> I knew it was the truth because my thoughts never sounded like that. My thoughts always criticized. This voice was kind.

After that day, I wasn't instantly twirled into a perfect woman like Cinderella before the ball. But I was different, more settled in my skin, and, dare I say it, happier. Knowing I was enough made me think about myself less. I was more able to focus on other people—home in on what they wanted and needed—rather than on the things I'd thought I needed to feel safe around them.

I got my degree, stuck it out for another few years, and then I heard that voice again. Almost audible. Completely unexpected. A name. My future husband's name. We weren't even dating, barely knew each other actually, and yet I knew. I knew this was the same voice that had told me I was enough, and now it was telling me this man would be enough for me. A tall order.

Wanting to stay home with my babies was a fabulous reason for never going back to nursing again. That was probably one of my greater gifts to humanity. And then I heard the voice one more time. Louder than a thought. Out of nowhere. *Thunk* into my soul. We would move to another country where we would be enough together.

We landed in Austin, Texas, with a three-year-old and a five-month-old and integrated quickly into a new routine of life. Gone were the days of dropping into a neighbor's house for tea unannounced. New was getting a driver's license and having to drive to go anywhere. We grew together; made friends; bought homes; raised our children; loved, laughed, and cried.

# Happiness Indeed

Sometimes we shed so many tears that we missed seeing the happy flashes for what they were—sparklers in the yard of life shooting hope into our dark moments and joy into our lighter ones.

And that voice ... God's. I like to think we are all created with a holding box that is opened by that voice, that presence, and once sprung open, we're released into all we can be. The stellar opposite of Pandora's box.

Married thirty-four years now, we have cycled through many efforts of finding what makes us feel fully alive, and we've found our finest happiness comes from moments when we can serve up our best from the fulness within—our special mix of Spirit, heart, talent, and hope. Our family has had so much to celebrate and look back on with joy, yet we also have so much beauty to stop and see and touch in the present. Yes, sitting in that old chair and hearing His voice say I was enough was one of my happiest moments, but in this season of my life, happiness holds new meaning.

Happiness isn't always about a moment in time I can never recapture. Sometimes it's about a truth given in a moment that takes root and grows in ways that allow it to be recaptured day after day forever. An infinite truth.

---

> Even if you sit in the exact same place and do *nothing* for the rest of your life, you are enough.

---

*Sally Hanan*

www.sallyhanan.com | www.inksnatcher.com

# Windows, Doors, and Jail Cells

## Michelle Carrier

If you have ever known the bond of longtime friendships, you understand what it is like to spend time apart, yet when you come back together, it is as if you pick up right where you left off. The bond remains strong and the value you have for each other grows through the ever-changing stories of your lives. Perhaps you have even found that a never-ending grace has been etched deep into your soul as your friends continue being friends when life gets wonky. Bill and I have been blessed with several lifelong friends. One of them is Michelle Carrier, whom I met in Bible college. Hear her story about facing failure and what is on the other side of it.

―∞―

I have always loved windows and doors. I love creating with them—from making tables to some type of décor out of them. When I look at these particular windows, they represent both joy and sadness, success and failure: joy in starting a new pathway that led us to step out and take a risk—by becoming entrepreneurs and starting our own business almost nine years ago, with several successful real estate investments—and sadness because we failed big time, not just a little, really bad, with some very significant loss.

## Windows, Doors, and Jail Cells

This threw me into a whirlwind of shame, doubt, insignificance, unsettling thoughts, and definitely never wanting to risk again. It was a daily battle to stand strong to God's Word and His promises and to trust the process and take risks again. So when looking at these windows, I understand that joy and sorrow will always coincide here on this earth, but it is up to us to choose how we are going to deal with it.

We still have not recovered from those losses, but I believe with all my heart that God is going to give us strategies and the ability to make all things right. So if you need to hear this:

> You may have failed, but that does not make you a failure!

Never doubt God's mighty power to work in you and accomplish all this. He will achieve infinitely more than your greatest request, your most unbelievable dream, and exceed your wildest imagination! He will outdo them all, for his miraculous power constantly energizes you. (Ephesians 3:20 TPT)

"I know the plans and thoughts that I have for you," says the LORD, "plans for peace and well-being and not for disaster, to give you a future and a hope. Then you will call on Me and you will come and pray to Me, and I will hear [your voice] and I will listen to you." (Jeremiah 29:11–12 AMP)

Do you see what this means—all these pioneers who blazed the way, all these veterans cheering us on? It means we'd better get on with it. Strip down, start running—and never quit! No extra spiritual fat, no parasitic sins. Keep your eyes on Jesus, who both began and finished this race we are in. Study how he did it. Because he never lost sight of where he was headed—that exhilarating finish in and with God— he could put up with anything along the way: Cross, shame, whatever. And now he is there, in the place of honor, right alongside God. When you find yourselves flagging in your faith, go over that story again, item by item, that long litany of hostility he plowed through. That will shoot adrenaline into your souls! (Hebrews 12:1–3 MSG)

## Michelle Carrier

Pure Legacy Farms
Instagram: pure_legacy_farms

——∞——

What a powerful encouragement from Michelle. As she shared her love for windows and doors, it made me think about the importance of perspective and how Jesus Himself is the door. "'I am the door; if anyone enters through Me, he will be saved, and will go in and out and find pasture'" (John 10:9). I believe there's a lot more to that verse than merely being saved. He makes Himself a living invitation that we can step into. When He spoke of being one, "On that day you will know that I am in My Father, and you are in Me, and I in you" (John 14:20), He was inviting us to step inside that reality.

Think of yourself in this moment, standing face-to-face with Jesus. See Him as the door, the living frame who beckons you to come. Come and step inside. See yourself merging into one with Him. When you do, your perspective changes because you now have the mind of Christ (1 Corinthians 2:16). He will fix your windows (your lenses) and He will give you the ability to see what He sees. You can bring your sorrow into that place and He turns it into joy.

Michelle shared the challenge that they faced with major financial loss, but that was not the only loss she and her family suffered. Imagine losing a child. And imagine that

## Windows, Doors, and Jail Cells

one of your other children ends up in jail. It is a story she knows personally, yet she continues to find God in each facet of that story. Doors and windows can represent many things. So can prison doors. Hear how the Father entered Michelle's daughter's life on a really bad day. Welcome, Kayla.

—∞—

Your GOD is present among you, a strong Warrior there to save you. Happy to have you back, he will calm you with his love and delight you with his songs. 'The accumulated sorrows of your exile will dissipate. I, your God, will get rid of them for you. You've carried those burdens long enough'" (Zephaniah 3:17–18 MSG).

Never did those words ring truer than when I woke up in a jail cell for the second time. The pastor's kid who had heard about God a million times but had chosen a different path. Who had spit in His face time and again. Who had no right to cry out to Him for help, or anything for that matter. Yet as I woke up with chaos and darkness and fear engulfing my entire being, the simple thought *Jesus, please* barely made its way into my mind. The most simple phrase. But in an instant, His tangible peace and presence filled every crevice of that jail cell and my being, and I could not deny Him anymore. I had chosen darkness! Yet He was there immediately, for me. I will never forget that moment—His love and desire for me even at my lowest and greatest distant from Him. There really is nothing that can separate us from the love of God, of that I am absolutely certain.

*Kayla Santos*

—∞—

Clearly there is no door that Jesus won't enter to save people. His love knows no barriers. Kayla now lives her life with her heart surrendered to God, and she walks with her husband and children into a legacy of faith that her parents have planted themselves in firmly. Kayla came to know God's love and faithfulness for herself. If you have children you are praying for, know that the Father loves them even more than you do. His nurturing hands and His words hold them no matter where they walk. Your prayers are powerful; their Maker is even more powerful to hold them and meet them along the path. His love knows no barriers.

# Walk On

### Shirley Peschell

Have you ever known someone whose inviting spirit makes you want to sit with them all day, listening to their stories? It is a special thing to have someone in your life who feels like a blanket of protection for the heart, soul, and spirit. I found that warmth in a woman named Shirley Peschell. She and her husband, David, have followed our ministry for several years, and we bonded over family challenges and stories of breakthrough. And let me tell you, Shirley knows breakthrough. She carries a fire and a tough edge wrapped in a tender, loving heart. She is a wife, a mother, and a former nurse with a profound strength and perseverance. I love the story she shared that encourages women to "walk on."

―∞―

Everyone looks for and finds encouragement in different ways. I was a ten-year-old girl growing up in Canada, facing overwhelming challenges with death, disease, and family troubles everywhere. Don't feel sorry for me. Everyone goes through issues. I know friends who sought encouragement through scholastic achievement, or athletics, or their circles of friends. Others just ran away unable to cope. My brother joined the Navy to escape his life. At ten years of age, I had no idea what the word "encouragement" meant. However, I found it in a movie, of all places.

Oscar Hammerstein wrote a song for the movie *Carousel* in 1956. I watched the movie as a ten-year-old. The end of the movie showed a young girl and her mother in the middle of grief while a schoolteacher encouraged the group to hold their heads up high. The lyrics talk about how we can hold our head up high no matter how bad things get, that we can always walk on with hope because we never walk alone, and that at the end of every storm is a golden dawn filled with peace.

Whenever I felt frightened or alone, I would sing this song to myself. Even now, after all these years of challenges, I listen to it and cry a little, but I know I have hope. A few years ago, Andrea Bocelli made a new music video of the song. His voice is exceptional, the video quality is excellent, and it is worthy of being called great. However, the voices from the movie in 1956 still echo to me, calling me with encouragement. Claiming not to know the answer to happiness, the schoolteacher and the group in the movie did just that to a ten-year-old girl, and they still encourage me today. I have hope and faith that the Lord is with me. With Him, everything is possible.

That old 1956 movie is no longer showing on the big screen, but some have preserved the most interesting final three minutes of that movie. You can view it on YouTube: www.youtube.com/watch?v=HQal2cBT39k.

Watch it. Sit with me in that darkened theater sixty-eight years ago and be encouraged. You are not alone. Walk on.

Shirley Peschell

# A Pause

### Regis Blalock

Here we are at the close of our time together at this virtual roundtable, and I have the privilege of introducing you to my baby sister, Regis. She is a woman who tackles life and is willing to take risks while also counting the costs. She is ready to pour out love and care to those God has placed in her life. She is a fierce lion and a steadying, nurturing force on this earth. I am so thankful for her. I find it to be beautifully appropriate that she sent me her nugget of wisdom at the tail end of this book because it is a great place to land. Carry her words with you and remember to pause each day. I will let her words bring this beautiful circle to a close, for now.

---

"Teach us to number our days, that we may gain a heart of wisdom" (Psalm 90:12 NIV). This is the verse that came to my mind as I prayed for wisdom for the coming school year. My calendar seemed to be filling faster than I could write down new entries. The pressure to check off outstanding items on my to-do list was mounting quickly.

Amid the feelings of stress, I paused. What did this verse really mean? In what areas of my life could I apply this? Surely there was wisdom to be gleaned. I began to ponder the answer. I realized that in this busy life, in the midst of personal pressures to perform well and promote ourselves and our self-interests, sometimes people distract us. That distraction can seem like an inconvenience, a feeling that they are getting in our way and preventing us from accomplishing important things. At times, this makes us react impatiently.

What we fail to realize is that the people who distract us may actually be our most important work—our calling to be human and to love. If we are mindful in numbering our days, perhaps it gives us the wisdom to pause and define what is actually important. What things or people deserve our attention beyond our pressure-ridden to-do lists? It gives us a reminder to pause and to not see the people in our lives as inconvenient distractions.

Love, and love well.

Regis Blalock

**Can You Help?**

Thank you for reading our book! We really appreciate feedback, and we would love to hear what you have to say.

Please leave us an honest review on your favorite bookstore sites letting others know what you thought of the book. Thanks so much!

*Traci Vanderbush*

# About the Author

Traci Vanderbush enjoys the simplicity of being married to her best friend and childhood sweetheart, Bill Vanderbush. She is mom to two amazing humans. Traci's passions are writing books and screenplays, dancing, exploring, and pursuing the Creator. She desires to bring hope to hearts of all ages through her writing. Certainly, every person has a dream deep inside, and Traci wants to see each person live his or her dream, no matter how big or small. A believer in redemption, she believes there is gold to be found in the most unlikely places.

**Websites**

www.theporchesofholly.com | www.tracivanderbush.com

**Facebook:** facebook.com/tracivanderbushwrites

**Twitter:** @tracivanderbush

**Instagram:** tracivanderbush

# Contributors

- Amber Twigg
- Becky Bird
- Bethany Martin
- Bettina Grzeskowiak
- Bonnie Goolsby
- Brit Eaton
- Britany Bloom
- Carrie Cole
- Celeste Keplin-Weeks
- Cheryl Ricker
- Christine Zucker
- Danielle Babin
- Eve Passmore
- Hannah Wakeman
- Jeanne Kaufman
- Jennifer Hart Shaw
- Katie Thorpe
- Kayla Carrier Santos
- Kayla Roberts
- Kerry Walker
- Kristin Tucker
- Libby Higgins
- Michelle Carrier

- Regis Blalock
- Robin Hertz Hempel
- Ronda Olson
- Ronda Vanderbush
- Sally Hanan
- Sarah Morales
- Shana Orser
- Shirley Peschell
- Stefanie Monk
- Stephanie Tate
- Tiffany Matthews
- Traci Vanderbush

# Acknowledgments

Special thanks to my husband, Bill Vanderbush, for his constant encouragement and empowerment to release the works and visions in my heart. Thank you to my children for being everlasting joys and cheerleaders when Mom is up to writing again.

I love you deeply, Bill, Britain, and Sara!

To every woman who contributed their stories and words; To every woman who came to the roundtable to share their voice, I cannot thank you enough! I value each of you greatly and I am eternally grateful to be surrounded by women in Christ who've gone through the fire and continued to shine their brilliant beauty brightly. I love you all.

# Other Books by Traci

Traci has created a variety of books for your enjoyment—from children's stories to life lessons, from fiction to nonfiction.

## Fiction

The Porches of Holly

The Windows of Holly

A Holly Christmas

## Nonfiction

The Four People You Marry

Into the Heart of Christmas

Soul Reformation

The Magic of our Forefathers

Walking with a Shepherd

## Children's Books

Mr. Thomas and the Cottonwood tree

Life with Lummox

Lummox and the Happy Christmas

Lummox and the Feast of Thanks

All books are available on Amazon and Barnes and Noble online, and also at tracivanderbush.wix.com/vanderbush.

Made in the USA
Monee, IL
25 February 2025